W9-BGK-715

THE FARM

THE
FARM

Life inside a
Women's Prison

Andi Rierden

University of Massachusetts Press
Amherst

LC 96-51511
ISBN 1-55849-079-5 (cloth); 080-9 (pbk.)

Designed by Dennis Anderson
Printed and bound by Braun-Brumfield, Inc.

Library of Congress Cataloging-in-Publication Data

Rierden, Andi, date.
  The farm : life inside a women's prison / Andi Rierden.
    p.   cm.
  Includes bibliographical references.
  ISBN 1-55849-079-5 (cloth : alk. paper). — ISBN 1-55849-080-9 (pbk. : alk. paper)
  1. Niantic Correctional Institution. 2. Reformatories for women—Connecticut. I. Title.
HV9475.C82N537   1997
365'.43'097465—dc21   96-51511
                                                               CIP

British Library Cataloguing in Publication data are available.

To Steven

People pay for what they do, and
still more, for what they have allowed
themselves to become. And they pay
for it simply: by the lives they lead.

—James Baldwin

Contents

Preface

My story about the Niantic Correctional Institution in Niantic, Connecticut, begins in the late 1980s and early 1990s, when I started writing articles as a freelancer for the *Sunday New York Times*. For the most part, my work as a journalist has focused on urban issues and crime reporting. Occasionally I've needed to take a breather and write about gardens or eccentric personalities, but I suppose it's an inner restlessness that has always drawn me back to the urban neighborhoods of New Haven and Bridgeport. Despite their troubles, such places possess a vitality and dimension not likely to be found in the suburbs. I had also lived and worked in the New Haven neighborhoods I later covered and had been an editor for a small newspaper in Bridgeport. From these vantage points, I was able to witness early on the slow decline of both cities.

I knew many families in the predominantly poor black and Hispanic sections of New Haven called the Hill and Newhallville. Both neighborhoods had marvelous histories as the assimilation points for new immigrants to the city. Most of the families I had known since the early 1980s who lived in these areas were hard working and full of promise. In 1985, I attended a barbecue in the Hill and recall hearing people from the neighborhood talk about this new drug, crack cocaine, that made you crazy. Indeed, after that, whole neighborhoods went crazy.

As a reporter covering those neighborhoods from 1989 to 1994, I witnessed dozens of youngsters I had known for years get swept up into the drug trade and subsequently make prison their second home. I was able to walk into precarious situations and interview drug bosses and gang leaders because I knew these kids and they knew and trusted me. Because I was friends with the "Ma" of one of those neighborhoods, I often heard dealers say to one another after I had appeared on the scene, "It's okay man, she's family." I had a gun pulled on me once, because I had walked into a bedroom unannounced and surprised the drug dealer sleeping there, who kept a handgun close to his pillow.

During those years, a lot of kids I had known killed someone, or else someone killed them. I did my last story in late 1994, about the murders of two friends. One boy died during a drive-by shooting, another was shot dead during a pointless argument over a bicycle. They are buried next to each other in the cemetery across the street from where they grew up, alongside the graves of other children whose lives were cut short by the culture of drugs and guns.

I had wanted to write a book about my experiences, but I felt Alex Kotlowitz covered the territory as well as anyone in his brilliant account of the Henry Horner projects in Chicago, *There Are No Children Here*. However, I felt that the one thing missing in the literature of the urban neighborhoods was the perspective of women. While I saw a lot of males dealing drugs on the streets, the women were often invisible. I saw more female drug addicts than men, and often when I asked about a certain young woman I hadn't seen for a while, I was told, nonchalantly, that she had gone on the "ho-stroll," that is, become a prostitute. I remember speaking to two young women on Davenport Avenue in the Hill, who had been in and out of Niantic more than a few times. They told me how easy it was to get high in jail and what a "hellhole" it was. I later ran into them while doing research for my book.

In 1992, I wrote an article for the *Times* on the issue of clemency for battered women. It included a woman in Niantic who was serving time for murdering her spouse and described how she hoped to receive a pardon (in Connecticut "clemency" is granted through the Board of Pardons, not the governor). While conducting interviews, I became intrigued by stories officials told me about "the Farm" (as Niantic is commonly called). I returned several weeks later and wrote an article about the prison's history.

The piece included interviews with two long-termers, Marie Rossignol and Delia Robinson. Robinson's presence and influence on inmates and some staff clearly marked her as one of the prison's matriarchs, a distinction I recognized during our first interview.

Frustrated with writing news analysis articles, which often seem too telescopic to give real depth and perspective to an issue, I wanted to continue the reporting I had started on the streets by pursuing a longer piece of writing on the women's prison. The new warden, Carol Dunn, gave me that opportunity. At first, she agreed to give me nearly unlimited access to inmates for just a couple of months. In all, I spent a total of about fourteen hundred hours inside the compound over the course of more than a year and a half.

Before I began my research I decided to make a contract with myself. Apart from the knowledge I had gathered as a crime journalist, I purposely limited my research beforehand because I felt it would affect my reporting. I did conduct an extensive bibliographic search on women in prison, putting aside several studies I felt might be helpful at a later date. I also read David J. Rothman's book *The Discovery of the Asylum*, and Susan Sheehan's *A Prisoner and a Prison*. From my reporting for the *Times*, I had already gathered the current statistics on women in prison regarding sexual abuse, drug addiction, and AIDS. Otherwise, I wanted to remain as untutored about my subjects as possible.

Though I was told by the warden that I would not have access to prisoners' records, I felt this was not an obstacle. The one thing I did have was plenty of time. I knew as a reporter that if you hang out long enough, eventually people reveal themselves to you in all manner of ways; something which was impossible to achieve in a typical news or feature story.

When it came to reporting styles, I tended to be old-fashioned and leaned a good deal on the proverbial "fly on the wall" model. Among its most astute practitioners was Henry Mayhew, the social historian and roving reporter whose renderings of the underbelly of Victorian London brought to life a world both shunned and ignored. In describing his book *The London Labour and the London Poor*, published in 1851, Mayhew called it "the first attempt to publish a history of a people from the lips of the people themselves—giving a literal description of . . . their trials and their sufferings in their own 'unvarnished' language. . . . to portray the condition of their homes and their families by personal observation of the places, and direct communion with the individuals." Like Mayhew, I too wanted to investigate a culture few journalists had explored in depth by simply standing back, remaining invisible, and letting people talk.

The myth of journalism is that the writer can transport events to a reader's mind without casting her shadow on them. To begin with, there arose some drawbacks in writing my account. Within a few months, I was known to most of the people in Niantic as the reporter or "lady writing a book on this place." This undoubtedly affected what I heard. Also, as a compact community tucked away on the Connecticut shoreline, the prison mirrored a small village where anonymity was simply impossible. What's more, as anyone who has lived in a small town split by various factions knows, if you do not form some allegiances you cannot engender trust. For my purpose, I needed to earn the trust of inmates so they would feel safe telling me things. At the same time, I had to earn the trust of administrators and correction officers (COs) so I could stay in the environment for as long as I felt was necessary. That proved, at times, to be a tricky balancing act.

I spent a good deal of time just hanging out with inmates, sometimes for five days a week, in their rooms, while they worked, ate, watched television, chatted with other inmates, participated in prison programs, or received counseling. In addition to my time spent with inmates, I interviewed close to a hundred people, including COs, counselors, schoolteachers, administrators, attorneys, and inmates' family and friends. Of the various scenes included in the book, I witnessed more than half. Those events at which I was not present, I pieced together from recollections of people who were. I relied on the prison's archives for historical background on the Farm, and on interviews with former wardens and staff.

When it came to recomposing stories for my text, sorting fact from fiction was rarely simple. I knew early on from COs that in prison "everything is magnified," and I assumed I would be getting some hefty doses of hyperbole. Therefore, in trying to discern the truth, I collected as many independent accounts as possible, including newspaper versions, which were often wilder than fiction. Because this book involves people who are incarcerated and therefore highly vulnerable, I made an effort to review thoughts and episodes with them many times, not only to ensure accuracy, but also to make certain the women felt comfortable including the material in the book. Because of the stigma of having a prison record, I changed the names of some inmates to protect their privacy.

One of the more contentious issues I confronted while conducting my research was that of sexual and physical abuse as a main factor in why women end up in prison. Though plenty of studies indicated that large numbers of women in prison had suffered earlier abuse (some as high as 85 percent), I still needed convincing. It was actually a topic I initially tried to avoid. I also did my research at a time when the issues of sexual abuse, false memory syndrome, and battered women's syndrome were saturating the talk shows and the print media (I did my own stories on these issues for the *Times*). Because of the amount of television inmates watched, I was concerned that it might sway what they told me. I ended up talking to several psychologists about their questioning methods, and about how they could determine whether someone had been abused, or was simply groping for an explanation for all her problems. I learned that although these professionals often had access to past psychological records, their methods did not appear that different from those of a good journalist. I came to my own conclusion that the truth in this matter of sexual and physical abuse was a highly elusive animal.

Still, the issue was pervasive at Niantic. And most everyone I spoke with—counselors, COs, and inmates—agreed with the statistics. One exception was Delia Robinson, who felt it was high, but that a lot of inmates leaned too heavily on the idea to explain their crimes.

I still do not know if the percentages of women in prison reported to have been sexually abused reflect the truth. However, I suspect that the numbers are not overly exaggerated. After observing dozens of inmates in formal and informal settings over the course of a year and a half, I can attest that for many, something, somewhere, in their lives went tragically awry. At times I was struck by the self-loathing and self-destructiveness of the personalities I encountered, many of whom never used the word "abuse." A lot of those women displayed the skittish wariness of animals who have been severely mistreated— the damage was embedded beyond reach. I have tried to portray this extreme loss of self in the stories of Cassandra and Justina.

I would also like to note that, like any community of human beings, Niantic harbored its share of good, bad, and indifferent. Some women had little intention of reforming themselves and basically exhibited the same behaviors in prison that they had while on the streets. Yet given the variety of inmates' personalities and situations, the population became impossible to drape in generalizations.

Often, however, I was stunned by comments people outside the prison system made to me either casually or in formal discussions about prisoners. I discovered on a number of occasions just how deeply entrenched are the myths and prejudices regarding incarcerated people. Even my mention of doing research in the prison was sometimes enough to trigger hostile remarks about "those people."

"Why can't those people in there be responsible citizens like me and my kids and most other people I know?" snapped one acquaintance, a suburban, single mother who had raised three children and was putting them through college. I had no clear answers or words of hope to ease her disappointment. What causes certain people to exhibit antisocial behavior is one of those great conundrums not likely to be solved soon, if ever. Throughout American history, theories on the matter have shifted with the tides of social change and political whim. In colonial times, Calvinists propounded the notion that crime in human beings was inherent, essentially the handiwork of the devil. Policymakers later decided that archaic laws and barbaric punishments carried over from the British system served to perpetuate deviancy. They then set out to amend criminal codes. After prison authorities in the Jeffersonian era began recording the histories of criminals through interviews, they concluded that deviancy had its roots in early childhood; a wrecked home life and corrupt environment could lead young people astray. Those sentiments led to the prison reform movements of the nineteenth and early twentieth centuries, and prevail to a large extent today.

Inmate Bonnie Foreshaw alludes to the "criminals are casualties of their environment" school of thought when she says to me in chapter 7, "So many of us here are victims of circumstance." Nowadays, mainstream America bristles at such phrases or any hint that a criminal might be leaning on the old "don't blame me" crutch. Given the egregious number of incidents in recent decades where victims of crimes and their families have continued to suffer at the hands of the criminal justice system and the media, those responses are clearly justified. However, I believe Foreshaw raises a key point regarding circumstance and one's destiny. The theme may be an old one, yet in seeking to understand criminal behavior, it should never be ignored.

For sake of argument, let me use my own life as an illustration. By the time I was thirteen, both of my parents had died and I spent my adolescence living in a boarding school and with friends. During those years, I was exposed to any number of circumstances that might have led to a life of crime. Somehow I avoided that route. I went to college, then graduate school, got married, and now lead what most would call a productive life. I suspect that my ability to transcend troublesome situations stemmed in part from the love my parents gave me and the values they instilled in me at a young age. It also had to do with the people I encountered and their influence on me and the fact that I experienced little economic instability. But to me, that is still conjecture. As an adolescent with boundless curiosity and no parental guidance, I could have gone in any number of directions. However, I happened to choose the ones that have led me to this moment. Though I would like to believe that my choices stemmed from some innate sense of responsibility, I frankly feel they had more to do with luck and circumstance than anything else.

While gathering information inside the prison, I was often stirred by the notion that I too could be sitting in one of those cottages, counting the days until my next parole hearing. Many people who work or conduct long-term research inside a prison will say the same thing.

The idea that we all possess the will to marshal our resources and triumph against all odds is a nice fantasy, but it is not realistic. The fact is, some of us make good responsible choices and some of us do not. When Foreshaw talks about the force of circumstance, she is speaking for many women in prison who, because of race, sex, economics, or a severely broken and damaged family life, end up in situations ripe for disaster. Put simply, a combination of factors can place a person at higher risk for trouble. It is no fluke that nearly half the women in prison today are poor and black, and that drug-related arrests for African American women increased 828 percent between 1986 and 1991. We live in a classist, racist, sexist society and nowhere is that more apparent than in a women's prison.

At the same time, I share the frustration of many people who feel that despite all the expense and care given to help those in "disadvantaged" situations, little progress has been made. Indeed, as Jonathan Kozol has said, it has gotten painfully worse. I often felt that some inmates were using their past as an excuse for the mess they had made of their lives. Instead of wallowing in self-pity, I would think to myself during a group counseling session or interview, wouldn't it be wiser to just get on with it? However, I was not there to reform inmates or the prison in which they lived. Nor was I there to retry inmates for their crimes. I basically wanted to record their stories and their actions within the prison culture, against the backdrop of several societal developments (AIDS, drug abuse, gangs, and so on). To do that I sought out inmates who might represent certain issues, and collectively, the majority of women in prison.

Furthermore, these stories are not meant to be the official records of what happened to the inmates. They are the personal testimonies of incarcerated women in which I have tried to unveil an internal as well as an external landscape. In doing so, I simply had to trust the integrity of my sources and my sense that people are usually the most credible witnesses to their own histories.

I would like to add that in the course of time I did develop biases. There were inmates and staff I grew to like and admire. Some of them became my best sources both on and off the record, and I relied on their knowledge of the prison to verify inmates' stories and to steer me to other people and situations. I would like to think that those connections made the manuscript better, not worse. In the same breath, I realized from the very beginning of my research that ultimately, the material I would gather over time would shape my narrative and point of view. There were certainly many books within the confines of the Farm. I wrote just one.

THE FARM

"A Prison with a View"

"With its private lake and wooded seclusion, the 895 acres of the Connecticut State Farm and Prison for Women at Niantic is one of the world's most unusual jails. There are no walls, no armed guards. . . . the whole country might well learn some valuable lessons from this small Connecticut prison."

This Week Magazine, June 26, 1966

Lieutenant Elizabeth Gilchrist is known around the Farm as an old blue shirt. She's worked as a guard here longer than anybody and can tell you just about anything you need to know. Young inmates fresh off the streets ask her, "Hey, you know my mother? You know my grandmother?" And likely she did or still does. Older long-termers say, "Beth? Oh me and her go back a long way." Most inmates agree, Gilchrist and COs like her are a dying breed. They'll tell you, "She's not like all these young COs comin' in here like they're on some power trip. That woman's got a good heart."

Nearly twenty-six years inside this place and she's showing little sign of world-weariness. She's seen entire families straggle in and out of here, and lately, entire neighborhoods. She's watched a procession of big-name researchers from Harvard and Yale come in and out of here, too, each possessing what everybody hoped might be the magic cure-all for criminal behavior. First came the behavior modification

1

and moral development phase, then came reality therapy, followed by meditation mixed in with art and nature therapy. Still, some of the women kept coming back, a lot of the same old faces and plenty of new ones too. Nowadays there is the whole co-dependency, acupuncture, twelve-step, empowerment thing. And why not, the Lieutenant will say, if we can help mend even a few lives it is worth the trouble. These people need all the help they can get.

Gilchrist has this steady, deadpan manner that either unnerves inmates or makes them feel at ease. You can't always tell where you stand with her. Still, many of the old-timers feel a kinship toward her; it sometimes gives the Lieutenant a conflicting feeling deep inside her chest, which she keeps to herself. One thing is for certain, she's nobody's yo-yo or duck. Some staff you can play to and spot their weaknesses. Before long, you've got them sneaking in meatball subs for you, and maybe a little Jack Daniels or who knows what else. Forget trying to bend Gilchrist, she's seen everything and is always about ten steps ahead of everybody.

If an inmate breaks the rules, Gilchrist doesn't let it slip. She'll call her into her office with the bay windows facing Bride Lake and the desk piled high with paperwork, where the phone rings nonstop and a half-eaten sandwich beckons and say, Have a seat. She'll take out her white pad as if she were about to jot down her grocery list, ask a few questions in her matter-of-fact monotone, then slap the rule breaker with a discipline.

To the Lieutenant, everybody is the same. You here for murder? For armed robbery? For spitting on the sidewalk? Doesn't matter. An inmate is an inmate is an inmate. That's that.

Well, not quite. "Some of these women just crack me up," she'll say if you press her. Or else she'll caution you to watch out for the swindlers. "Believe you me," she'll say, like someone who knows what she's talking about, "we've got our share of classic con artists."

These days, the Lieutenant spends most of her time making certain the 110 women in the cottage she oversees are accounted for. Trying to rehabilitate these people in light of everything else going on seems next to impossible. When she first came here the entire prison housed a hundred women. It was nice and cozy then, every inmate had her own room. She knew everybody's name and the names of her kids, boyfriends, husband, mother, father, brothers, sisters, and friends. These days, the Lieutenant just wants to make certain all the women the courts keep unloading here get a bed, or at least a mattress on the floor. These days, she writes enough disciplines to fill Bride Lake. Everybody's getting on everybody's nerves. There are more drugs, more assaults, and now AIDS and gangs. These days, the Lieutenant often thinks back to when she spent most of her time with a handful of inmates trying to decide whether to take them fishing or to sit with one of them and have a nice long chat. These days, all that seems like a distant dream.

The bigger picture. During the 1980s the numbers of women in American prisons and jails had tripled and Niantic was no exception. By 1991, the population at Niantic had risen to 606, a 159 percent increase from ten years before. Across the country, it was the same story.

The reason behind the explosion came down to one word: drugs. The federal and state crackdown on the sale and use of narcotics caught many women in the dragnet. Mandatory minimum sentencing laws passed during the War on Drugs era of the late 1970s and early '80s resulted in more punitive responses to these crimes. The lack of viable outside treatment centers and alternative sanctions for women also contributed to the increase. During this time, the number of women arrested for drug offenses went up 89 percent compared with 51 percent for men. Offenses related to drug use like prostitution and theft also escalated. Studies showed that women were more likely than men to use drugs, and to use more serious drugs with greater frequency.

In the span of a decade, prisons and jails nationwide, which had witnessed a slow and steady rise in female inmates since the turn of the century, became overwhelmed with unprecedented numbers of women, whose lifestyles, family histories, and drug abuse had scarred more than a few of them with multiple mental and physical health problems.

In Connecticut, a host of changes in prison policy beginning in the early 1990s further complicated the overcrowding problem. Influenced by the tougher trends regarding punishment, new standards required inmates to serve 50 percent of their sentences, up from 14 percent. The state also cut back on "good time," the days off of a sentence that a prisoner receives for good behavior. Other developments included phasing out the supervised home-release program, which had been considered a safety valve for managing overcrowding. The resulting mayhem turned the state's only women's prison into a pressure cooker. Built for a much smaller and more docile population, Niantic began to resemble a repository more than a reformatory. In the midst of it all stood Gilchrist and a handful of other Niantic veterans who knew the center could not hold for too much longer. Without a question, things were falling apart.

Yet in the spring of 1992, lists of statistics and laments about the rising numbers of female prisoners isn't something the Lieutenant has the time or even the inclination to ponder. Like an old warrior who refuses to retreat from the front lines, her response to the chaos is more instinctual than academic. She's uncertain what the next few years will bring. The Department of Correction (DOC) has just broken ground for a high-tech prison to house Niantic's maximum-security crowd. Perhaps the new building will relieve the population crunch and allow Gilchrist and the rest of the staff to get back to the basics of helping inmates. Perhaps not.

When I first began my eighteen-month journey inside the Farm, Gilchrist was my tour guide. From the beginning, when she first met me in the prison's Visitors' Center, it was clear she had insight and an attachment to the place that anyone new to Niantic could not begin to glean. As she approached me, inmates in the center hollered greetings to her and their family members did too. Dressed in a uniform of gray slacks and a white lieutenant's shirt branded with gold and blue stripes above her name tag for "outstanding meritorious service," Gilchrist simply nodded to them or raised her hand slightly like some laid-back deputy sheriff. On one hip hung a clump of keys and on the other, a walkie-talkie. She had a solid build and kept her brown hair cropped short. Her face was round and handsome, lightly freckled and accented by blue-gray eyes. As we shook hands, she displayed a reserve about her which bordered on shyness. "So what can I do for ya?" she said, with a steady but uncertain gaze.

Carol Dunn, the new prison warden, had asked her to give me a tour of the grounds and to talk to me about the prison's history. According to the warden, few knew more or cared more about Niantic than Lieutenant Gilchrist.

The entrance to the Farm faces Main Street in Niantic, a section of the town of East Lyme, on the Connecticut shoreline, between the

Connecticut and Thames rivers. The state's tourism office has coined this corner of Connecticut the nautical southeast. East of Niantic, Mystic Seaport and the surrounding maritime towns attract a large chunk of the state's annual tourist trade. To the north in Ledyard, the Mashantucket Pequots own one of the world's largest and most profitable casinos. The region's landscape is hilly and pastoral, lined with Victorian homes, ranch houses, and a few Greek Revival mansions left over from the state's whaling days. Named after a Pequot Indian tribe, Niantic rests quietly on the coastline. Its premier attraction is Rocky Neck State Park, which lies across the road from the prison and down a few hundred yards. The park faces Long Island Sound and contains a mile-long crescent beach, a boardwalk, and concession stands, making it a popular spot for families.

From the road turning into the prison, the only visible structures are an old brick administration building (ADM) and the more modern Visitors' Center. To get beyond, visitors must first be cleared inside ADM by signing into a thick ledger and showing some identification. If okayed, they receive a clip-on pass. From there, they go back to the front parking lot, drive up to a metal gate on the side of ADM, honk their horn until the CO on duty hears it and acknowledges them, pressing a button inside to open the gate. Depending upon the level of the day's congestion, the process can take up to thirty minutes. Sometimes the gate works and sometimes it doesn't. Often it's left opened all day because of a malfunction.

After Gilchrist introduces herself, she leads me through a back door of the Visitors' Center into the prison grounds. To the east lies a meadow of several acres lined with woods and a two-mile stretch of road looping around the grounds and leading to the Farm's housing hub. It is a lovely site. Spring wildflowers carpet the landscape in rich pinks and yellows, and the air smells sweet with a mixture of pine and clover. As we slide into her blue Ford station wagon parked in back of ADM, Gilchrist tells me that inmates had spotted a coyote darting across the field earlier in the day. "But it was probably a red fox," she says.

Wildlife is all around, she adds. Deer, fox, possums, raccoons, waterfowl. She breaks into a proud grin and nods when I comment about the Farm's natural beauty. "Most of these women here come from the cities and have never been in a setting like this," she says. "All they've known is concrete and traffic."

The scenery has changed little since 1966, when Gilchrist first visited the prison farm. To the twenty-three-year-old Maryland native, arriving here was like reaching the end of a long pilgrimage. For some time she had been working at a residential home for emotionally disturbed boys outside Baltimore and was aching to do more with her life. One day she picked up a Sunday supplement out of the *Baltimore Sun* and spotted an article titled, "A Prison with a View," about this prison for women in Connecticut. The article examined the regimen at Niantic, with its campuslike atmosphere, where inmates spent their time in "unprison-like activities" such as going to school and attending group therapy and Alcoholics Anonymous. It also pointed out that only 10 percent of Niantic's "graduates" once released from parole became lawbreakers again, compared with a national average of 30 percent. Warden Janet York, whose innovative programs were attracting researchers and observers from all over the country, said in the article that the main goal of the facility was to teach inmates how to "live properly."

"Somehow, somewhere, I think we manage to reach every girl in some way—give each a feeling that there is such a thing in this world as love and hope," York is quoted as saying. "When you start to do that, the crime rate is bound to fall."

The article changed Gilchrist's life. "I called Warden York as soon as I could and asked her if I could visit," she says. "When I got here, I couldn't believe it. This place didn't look at all like a prison, it looked like a picture postcard. The meadow was filled with all sorts of vegetables—tomatoes, corn, strawberries, about anything you could imagine. Warden York asked if I'd come to work here that day. She was a little concerned that I wouldn't like the schedule and routine. But I had no problem at all. This was the place I wanted to be."

Opened in 1918 during the Progressive Era of prison reform, the Connecticut State Farm and Prison for Women, as it was called until the late 1960s, was one of the first women's reformatories in the country (led by the Northeast, seventeen reformatories opened between 1900 and 1935). Built in response to a series of campaigns starting in the mid-1800s against the rise of sexual immorality, the reformatories were located in rural areas to isolate young women, many of whom were prostitutes, from the corruption of city life and to provide outdoor exercise that might aid in restoring them to physical and moral health. As the country's first prisons for women, the reformatories broke away from the male model by keeping the grounds unwalled and shunning large-scale congregate buildings. Instead, the women's reformatories embraced the "cottage" plan, housing small groups of women in handsome quarters where they could live with a motherly matron in a family setting. With its wooded terrain and open pastures, Niantic embodied the ideal female reformatory.

When Gilchrist was hired, prison guards at the Farm were still called matrons, and the absence of any affirmative action policies ensured the prison's original intent as a village of women. Like her predecessors, Gilchrist lived in one of the cottages around the clock, five days a week. As the youngest matron, she had a difficult time breaking into the well-established clique of her colleagues. It took several months for the icy welcome she received to thaw. Gilchrist tells me she didn't mind though; even then she knew she'd found the place where she hoped to devote her life's work.

Her day started at 4:30 in the morning. She sent women into the vegetable fields and orchards, or to the dairy barns and hen houses. "We put them to bed at night, then got them up in the morning," Gilchrist recalls as we drive toward the cottages. For recreation she took them fishing or swimming in the prison's lake, or off-grounds to a restaurant or to hear a classical concert. There were also pageants, picnics, and holiday parades on the prison grounds.

Gilchrist tells me the story of one Christmas in the late '60s when the inmates put on an elaborate nativity play. "The Three Kings were played by these three alcoholics," she says, chuckling at the irony. To achieve a realistic effect, the women shredded sanitary napkins and used the stuffing for beards.

Once past the meadow, we drive into the parking lot of the Janet S. York Dormitory, the latest addition to the prison and the first housing unit built since the 1940s. Constructed in 1988 to hold 104 inmates, the dormitory was designed to relieve the prison's overcrowding. On this day, it holds double that amount. York is a glaring symbol of the crisis consuming Niantic and other women's prisons. Inside, the air is stagnant, smelling of stale cigarettes and sweat. The poor fluorescent lighting and drab yellow walls give everyone a jaundicelike pallor. Inmates have dubbed this breeding ground for drug trafficking, assaults, and gang activity, "Calcutta." Wall-to-wall women, and the noise level is deafening.

Gilchrist introduces me to Lt. Anthony Colonus, a garrulous twenty-year veteran of Niantic, who wastes no time telling me how bleak things are and how much bleaker they are going to get. Gilchrist tells him she has been talking to me about the old days.

"Let me tell ya somethin'," Colonus says, leaning into my face. "This place used to be beautiful. When I first came here in the 1970s there were 120 inmates. Now with this whole drug thing it's a mess."

He leads me through some metal doors into the south side of the dormitory. There, more than a hundred women are stacked four to eight per cubicle, some with their legs dangling off upper bunks, some sleeping, many wearing a thick lackadaisical cast.

"When I first came here," Colonus says, "the inmates were all working outdoors, doing something. Then the state took the farm thing away, the population exploded leaving most of these people with nothing to do. Here we have the result."

As he walks me back to the commons area, the lieutenant says half-jokingly, "I think maybe now's the time to retire."

Back inside her station wagon, Gilchrist doesn't add much about the nightmare of York dorm; it is as if the building stands for some family scandal she prefers not to discuss. As we drive deeper into the prison's original grounds, the scene becomes more placid. A half mile down the road, shaded by a canopy of pines, dogwoods, and maples, lies the ensemble of two-story Georgian brick cottages that have retained some of their 1930s majesty. The cottages look out over Bride Lake, a pristine seventy-three-acre preserve, where, I am told, inmates of the early days used to get married.

When the prison first opened, it did so with barely a game plan. With only a few farm buildings, the prison had scarce space for classrooms and workrooms. By 1925 it experienced its first overcrowding and disciplinary crisis. "Many of the women are psychopathic," a prison report from the period exclaimed. Unlike other Progressives who founded reformatories, the Farm's founders handled not only wayward women, but also dozens of criminals from the local jails. Repeated appeals to the state legislature by prison reformers eventually garnered the financing to build and open the five cottages. The Farm finally stabilized in the 1930s, under the guidance of Elizabeth Munger, a internationally recognized penologist and leading advocate of rehabilitating prisoners by altering their behavior. As the Farm's third superintendent, Munger remained true to the progressive spirit by introducing many reform programs, revamping the administration, and introducing an effective classification system for inmates. Her approach to prison management was featured in newspaper and magazine articles throughout the country, and placed her in great demand internationally as a speaker on penal issues.

The women in Niantic are housed in a system similar to the one Munger devised. Fenwick cottage shelters long-term inmates in one wing and young offenders in the other. Trumbull cottage next door is used for general housing of sentenced women. Across the road, Thompson Hall holds high-bond, pretrial inmates on one side and segregated inmates on the other. Lucretia Shaw, off a side road nearest to the lake, was formerly used as the sewing building and is now undergoing renovation.

The four buildings were named after prominent women with strong ties to the state or to prison reform. Most were built by WPA crews between 1932 and 1938. Each of the cottages has its own particular culture, Gilchrist tells me. Fenwick South and Thompson Hall, for instance, "are as different as night from day."

The enclave of buildings includes Davis Hall, the prison's medical and mental health unit, built in the 1920s. Behind the Fenwicks stands the old schoolhouse, still in use, and the Eleanor Little Chapel, named after a former state representative and prison reform advocate who served on the prison's board of directors until 1969. To the north of the school, there are a couple of greenhouses and a barn left over from the farming days. All in all, the original grounds have a restful feel about them. Inmates stroll the area with ease, on their way to and from the medical unit, school, or Visitors' Center. One woman powerwalks around the loop of the prison, wearing a Spandex outfit and a bandanna. Jogging, Gilchrist informs me, is permitted only within the fenced recreation yards.

In the back room of a small brick building holding inmates' property, Gilchrist leads me to a wooden table cluttered with Niantic's past: hats, T-shirts, coats, letters, and books left behind by inmates and staff. Though most of the materials resemble items from a rummaging table at the Salvation Army, Gilchrist hands me a couple of gems. One scrapbook from the 1940s meticulously documents the film career of Ingrid Bergman, replete with magazine photos, reviews, and exposés. Gilchrist pulls out a box from another corner filled with photographs of the old Farm days. The sepia-toned images show inmates working in the fields under a pillowy sky, at play, and sewing. Gilchrist handles the artifacts with the care of a museum curator.

While I sit and thumb through the items, she paints a sweeping profile of the Niantic inmates: women who have typically come from poor, urban neighborhoods. Many are poorly educated and learning disabled due to the effects of fetal alcohol syndrome or their own addictions. A lot of the women do not know what to make of living in the boondocks. But once they adapt, it is not uncommon for some to think of it as the best and safest home they have ever known. It is a place they don't want to leave when their time runs out.

In the 1970s Gilchrist often took groups of inmates off-grounds to a restaurant, something she would never be allowed to do now. Once at a seafood place in nearby Mystic, an inmate carried out a plant from the dining room and Gilchrist had to explain to her that that was not permissible. Another time, an inmate got in the car after they had eaten dinner and handed Gilchrist the tip that she had left on the table for the waitress. "Here, you forgot your money," the inmate said to Gilchrist. "The woman had little knowledge of social courtesies," Gilchrist says. "Most inmates grow up in these neighborhoods and never go beyond. Most of them couldn't even find this place on a map."

Of the thousands of inmates Gilchrist has seen come and go, a few keep resurfacing in her memory. In 1979, Gilchrist started a program called Project RAP, which involved taking inmates to speak to high school students and youth groups to dissuade them from committing crimes. One of her first Project RAP participants was an enthusiastic young woman named Felicia. Gilchrist had high hopes for the woman. "She was beautiful and funny and often dreamed about becoming a journalist. Yet she kept on coming back here for years on drug convictions."

In the mid-80s, while still under the charge of the Department of Correction, Felicia died in a local hospice. "We later realized she died from AIDS, but at the time nobody knew anything about it," says Gilchrist. "As far as we know, she became the first inmate from Niantic to die from the disease." There's a sadness in Gilchrist's recollection. She dwells for a few more seconds on what she's just said, then adds with Sisyphean acceptance: "As much as we try, once they leave here there's not much we can do."

Gilchrist packs away the photos and scrapbook and we head out to her car. She is much more ruminative. Niantic was never meant to be a panacea for society's problems, she explains, almost like an apology. She stands with her back to the field where inmates once harvested their crops, where the DOC has recently broken ground for the new prison. "I used to think that there was something I could say or do to change people's lives," she continues. "But I've come to learn that human nature is a far too complicated matter. We've always been like a small town and I've always been open to new ideas that might help someone. Sometimes they work, sometimes they don't. But we always keep trying. And that's why I stay here, and that's what I love about this place."

That same day, Gilchrist introduces me to the two inmates who have been in and out of Niantic the longest. They both live in Fenwick South, the most stable of the cottages. Marie Rossignol has the distinction of being one of the last women in the state to be sent to Niantic for "manifest danger of falling into vice," and "lascivious carriage," euphemistic terms for having sex and for getting pregnant out of wedlock. She's now recovering from a bad cocaine habit and serving a twenty-year sentence for robbery.

When she was first sentenced to the Farm on a three-year bid, Rossignol got up at the crack of dawn and polished eggs in the hen house. "It was a completely different scene then," she tells me as we sit in the Visitors' Center. She has soft curly brown hair and wears thick glasses. "The food was delicious because we grew it here. The manual labor was pleasant, and everybody knew everybody. There were no bars on the windows and no razor-wire fences."

The two laws Rossignol was accused of violating were declared unconstitutional by the late 1960s, but before then thousands of women in the state had served terms for similar convictions. Rossignol says she has no idea if being thrown in prison at such a young age for a such a preposterous crime had anything to do with her repeated criminal behavior. She has a simple, jocose way about her that does not seem prone to psychoanalytic meanderings. She tells me she had run away from home as a child after she found out her father was actually her stepfather. She became addicted to drugs in the '70's and went into a methadone program for a while. In the '80's, it was cocaine. She shoplifted to support her habit and started breaking into and robbing houses at night.

"I used to think that if somebody blew me away they'd be doing me a big favor," Rossignol says with little trace of self-pity.

Her drug habit and lifestyle have ravaged her health. Now in her early forties, she is plagued by diabetes, which sometimes forces her to walk with a cane. She has lost a son to foster care, and hopes to get him back one day. In Niantic she is considered one of the best key-punch operators and she keeps herself busy with needlework and correspondence courses.

The other inmate Gilchrist introduces me to, Delia Robinson, is known around the Farm as Miss D. She lives down the hall from Rossignol in Fenwick South and is serving a sentence for man-slaughter. Gilchrist has alerted her ahead of time of my coming. At Fenwick South, we find her listening to gospel music in her room and preening herself in front of a small mirror. A stack of crossword puzzles rests on her bed.

"You know I don't talk to anybody before I have my shower," Robinson quips, making Gilchrist chuckle.

"Don't worry, D., she's a nice person."

Robinson looks me up and down with cordial suspicion. "I know you wouldn't send me anybody mean."

At that, she asks me to have a seat on her bed. Gilchrist backs out of the tiny room saying she'll be back in a few minutes. She closes the door behind her. Within minutes Robinson and I find some common ground. I learn she has lived in New Haven for most of her life. We both know or know of reverends, shopkeepers, and notorious characters mostly from the predominantly black Dixwell-Newhall-ville section. She grew up in the era of urban renewal and has a wide grasp of the city's bumpy contemporary history. I spend some time catching her up on what is going on in the neighborhoods.

"I'm just glad I'm out of there," she says.

Once we get around to the topic of Niantic, I sense she wants to keep things on the lighter side and just talk about the prison's history. She confirms everything that Rossignol has said about the old days and adds other fascinating anecdotes about her cooking and fishing escapades. Overall, she hates how the prison is changing, but feels grateful to be living in Fenwick South, the prison's one remaining oasis. Through innuendo she makes it clear that her life has been yanked around and stomped on more than a few times, but that she in turn has committed her share of horrific misdeeds. During our first interview, I recognize without much difficulty that Delia Robinson wields a lot of clout. As we talk, a line of women stand outside her door waiting to see her. The CO on duty checks in on us a few times, as if she is afraid the interviewer may say something to upset the inmate. I have no cause to, and know better.

Some forty-five minutes later, Gilchrist reappears. "That woman knows how to bake a good sweet potato pie," she says about Robinson, who responds with a deep laugh. They apparently go back a long way.

While Gilchrist chats with inmates, Robinson and I say goodbye. I tell her I would like to talk to her further sometime. She obliges, then whispers intensely, "A lot of these women will tell you all sorts of reasons why they're in here. But I'll tell you right now that I'm in here by no fault but my own."

Driving back to ADM I ask Gilchrist what Robinson's manslaughter charge entailed. She mulls it over a second, then turns away from me and looks straight ahead. With a hesitancy she mumbles, "It had something to do with her son."

After that first day, I went home and wrote about the Farm's history for the *New York Times'* Connecticut Weekly section. The article featured a spread of photographs of inmates from the early days and of Marie Rossignol in her room crocheting. Delia Robinson asked not to be photographed. A month later I returned and began collecting what would amount to a couple of hundred pages of research and interview notes. During that time, I saw Lieutenant Gilchrist only sporadically. The population "crunch" and the chain reaction of unprecedented problems that arose as a result, had swamped most of the administrators in a tangle of paper work and responsibilities that gave them little time for casual conversations.

Most of the time, I was on my own. I went in and out of cottages and dormitories with few clearance problems and without a CO watching over my shoulder. When I could cull a few moments from staff, I found them eager to talk with me and provide their own point of view. At times I felt those conversations provided them with some relief from all the stress overcrowding had imposed.

Early on, one thing became clear. The portrait of the Farm that Gilchrist had presented was in its last vestiges. The old progressive spirit that had reigned for decades, albeit in different variations, had slowly and painfully dimmed to a flicker. Niantic in the early 1990s was like a once snug little town steeped in tradition and culture that had been forced to undergo urbanization. With a new "confinement model" prison rising from the earth and the threat of a less sympathetic political climate upstream, the atmosphere seemed foreboding. No one could say for certain what lay ahead.

PART

1

"In prison everything is magnified.
It's like a child's world."

—Rebecca Coutu, correction officer

1

Miss Delia of Sleepy Hollow

On a rainy summer morning, Miss Delia Robinson lies clutching her Bible and watching the blue light of her television flicker on the walls of her compact room in Fenwick South. Trembling from the icy grip of a high fever, the fifty-nine-year-old matriarch fixes her eyes on the picture of Jesus Christ pasted above her TV and whispers over and over. "Don't take me now, dear Jesus. Not now."

The alarm clock on top of her wardrobe ticks away at about 2:15 A.M., though it feels much later. She closes her eyes tight and prays hard. Her breathing grows heavier. The tingling sensation in her hands, arms, and legs feels like a cavalry of ants is scurrying beneath her skin. She's spent a total of twelve years inside this prison, and the more she thinks about the possibilities of dying here, the more her sensations intensify. True, she's made good, honest friends here—she calls them her daughters and sisters—but this will never be home. Home is maybe New Haven or New London or Granite Quarry, North Carolina, but never Niantic, the place most of the inmates and staff refer to as the Farm, because of its early origins as a prison-run farm.

She hears a door creak open down the hall and a sleepy shuffle to the bathroom. Must be Katie or Lori, Miss Delia thinks, hoping that either one might sense her pain and come to her door. Delia waits until she hears the toilet flush, then considers crying out to whomever is out there, but decides against it.

17

"I don't need no help from nobody, anyway," she whispers to herself. The thought makes her smile because that's what her grandfather, Thomas Jefferson Ruff, might have said, and that's where she gets her grit. His presence still pulses through her life forty-five years after her family buried him in a valley grave plot near Granite Quarry. The image of his alabaster beard, his tall sinewy build, and the sound of his brazen voice as he read from Genesis or Ecclesiastes every morning before she left for school, still rage inside her, especially in times of trouble.

Now, years later, as she lies sick in a place she never imagined she would be, all those early memories rush through her mind like the blur of the roadside through the window of a train: Daddy Ruff's smokehouse out back that she had made into a playhouse; the smell of granite dust and sweat that clung to Daddy after he returned from working in the quarries; the "piccolo" club in the backwoods with a still full of moonshine always beckoning to her; the summer Daddy got sick with dropsy, and how she had nursed him until he died.

The tingling in her limbs makes her flail her wrists into the air in an attempt to set the flow of blood straight. She feels delirious. Through the fog of fever she hears the door to her wing swing open and the familiar jingle of keys tapping against the pant leg of a correction officer making her rounds. The static bark of the officer's two-way radio crashes through the night silence.

As an inmate Delia just accepts those annoyances. After all, this is a prison, not a Holiday Inn, the guards often tell the inmates who complain. Then they add: "If you didn't do the crime you wouldn't have to do the time." Delia has a hard time tolerating inmates who forever complain. As far as she is concerned, they make it worse for everybody.

She especially disdains those troublemakers who live in the other, short-term cottages. These are the people who shuffle in and out of the prison gates like they were turnstiles. They come in off the streets looking like zombies, bone thin and strung out on crack cocaine or p-dope. "You can tell them by the abscesses on their bodies from shooting liquid dope cut with meat tenderizer," Delia notes.

Before long these inmates fatten up on the prison's starchy food and the junk they order from commissary, smuggle in drugs, and sleep around with women, even though they likely have a boyfriend or husband on the outside. Once released, they'll return to the streets, get arrested, and then return to the Farm. Once settled in they'll unite with old flames and "just chill."

"Those people make me sick," Delia tells me time and time again. "They're nothin' but a bunch of scrounges."

Delia came to the Farm for the first time in the late 1960s, on a manslaughter charge. The victim was a woman who had had a baby with Delia's brother. She and the woman spent one evening drinking, playing cards, and arguing. "She was a prostitute and always getting into fights with everybody," Delia recalled. Things escalated and in the fury Delia stabbed the woman to death. There had been assault charges in the past, but nothing so serious as this.

She arrived at the Farm half-mad. They placed her in Davis Hall's mental health unit and gave her tranquilizers and counseling. Then they sent her out to work in the kitchen washing trays and serving food. As always, work was her tonic. She despised idleness. After about a month, they placed her in Thompson Hall, because of her high bond. There she scrubbed the floors, washed the windows and walls, anything to keep her mind busy and give herself a sense of worth.

When the Black Panthers were thrown into Niantic on murder and extortion charges in the early 1970s, a number of inmates rallied to their defense and threatened to stage a sit-in to protest conditions at the prison. But Delia would have nothing to do with prison politics. "I never could understand why anyone would want to cause trouble for themselves. I was there to do my time and that was that."

Back then the Farm held around a hundred women. Most of the cottages were left unlocked and inmates could roam the grounds with little supervision. After Delia received a sentence of seven years, she was moved to the Trumbulls where she met Bobbie Moore, eight years her junior and her polar opposite. Bobbie's hardball humor and tall tales from the streets of Hartford kept Delia and other inmates highly amused. Before long, the two women became good friends.

As a fellow southerner, Delia admired Bobbie's backcountry acumen, particularly her fishing skills. Once the weather warmed, the women scavenged a couple of fishing poles made of bamboo and string and walked along the banks of Bride Lake, divining the best spots to catch fish. Then Bobbie waded into the lake until the water crept up to her waist. She stuffed grouper, pike, bass, or whatever else she caught into her underwear, then waded back to shore after she had accrued a full house. The women would toss their bounty into a metal bucket and haul it back to the small kitchen in the Fenwick cottage. Over a great gas stove, Delia would fry the fish crisp in a batter of lard, cook up some boiled collards, corn on the cob, and fruit pies and serve them to the inmates and staff on picnic tables overlooking the lake.

Delia returned in 1977 on an assault charge and picked up where she had left off. She got her old job back at the local convalescent home where she had worked as a cook, and continued to prepare meals for inmates and staff. Little had changed.

But when Delia returned in 1985, she found a different place indeed. The population had grown sevenfold, and most of the new breed of inmates were addicted to opiates. Security was tighter. The doors to the cottages were locked at all times. Inmates could no longer fish in the lake and swimming was closely supervised.

By then the prison had completely phased out the farm program. The expense of the enterprise and an emphasis on more contemporary approaches to rehabilitation eventually led to its demise.

The absence of farming as a rehabilitative measure created, in part, a situation ripe for inmate idleness. Inmates throughout the prison filled the time void by stationing themselves in front of the television or holing up in their rooms to dwell on their dismal circumstances.

Others created their own drug operations by smuggling in cocaine, heroin, and marijuana through the Visitors' Center or with inmates returning from furloughs. The drug trade spurred sporadic room searches led by a group of guards the inmates called the goon squad. Even house plants were confiscated after officials discovered that the potting soil made an ideal spot to hide drugs. Delia, who loved to decorate her room with cuttings of coleus and ivy, was told one day to move her plants outdoors or onto the back porch.

Regardless of all the craziness, as she calls it, Delia feels blessed. For the past seven years she has lived in Fenwick South, the homiest and most peaceful of all the cottages. Most of the inmates on her floor are in for murder, manslaughter, robbery, or assault. Because it's the cottage for long-termers, the women here treat it like home; plants on the front door step and screened side porch, and ruffled curtains on many of the inmates' windows. There's respect for one's privacy. It's the cottage Warden Dunn prefers to visit when she's showing state officials around the prison, because it's nearly always spotless.

Situated on a grassy patch facing Bride Lake, the Fenwicks have a stately appearance, at least from the outside. Inside, the building is divided like a huge duplex and the unit on the north side differs radically from the one on the south, both in appearance and clientele. Long ago, Fenwick South acquired the moniker of Sleepy Hollow because of its subdued nature. Unlike those who live on the northside, the women sent here are typically much older and have lived a life full of family and responsibility before their arrests.

Wayne Keck, a counselor at Fenwick South, considers the women under his charge atypical of other inmates. "These are not your troublemakers," says the former army chaplain as he sits in his office near the front entrance of the cottage. "These are people who, because of the nature of their crimes, go day-to-day with the pain. Many of these women still have feelings for the people they killed."

Keck refers to himself as Major Dad, a title some of the women find offensive. But he and Delia hold a deep respect for one another. Sometimes, if a matter erupts in the cottage that threatens to cause disharmony, he'll talk first with Delia, to get a clear picture of the situation before deciding what to do. She is by no means a snitch, but rather has a solid grasp of the surrounding culture and is always able to shed some common sense on most situations. Delia, in turn, places a lot of faith in Keck's abilities, and for that he is grateful.

"The hardest thing for a male counselor is to gain trust," he tells me. "Many of these women have been abused and the moment you reach out you get a strange reaction. My biggest challenge is to convey to them that not all males are the same."

Many of the women in Fenwick South work hard to send money to their families on the outside. They hold jobs in keypunch, commissary, or assist teachers at the prison school. For those who've exhausted what education programs the prison has to offer, correspondence schools in subjects as diverse as paralegal studies and veterinary medicine become their only option. The more motivated collect the certificates and diplomas like baseball cards.

As one of the oldest and most respected long-termers, Delia has nurtured a large extended family within the prison, made up of "daughters" and "granddaughters," "sisters" and "aunts." Her home, one of two single rooms in Sleepy Hollow, glows with hospitality.

Painted a pale blue, it measures about seven by twelve feet with a window at one end, next to her television. The red cedar tree standing outside her window shades the sun, making the room the coolest in the building. Atop her wardrobe sit colorful stuffed animals crocheted for her by an inmate who has left the prison and another young woman, one of her adopted daughters, who has died of AIDS. Her favorite animal is a powder blue parrot perched in a cage, which hangs from her ceiling. She calls it Mr. Tweetie Bird. Each month, like clockwork, she takes the bird and the cage down and washes them in a large basin across the hall inside the janitor's closet, removing any smells or stains from cigarette smoke.

At least twice a week she scrubs the linoleum floor of her room until it gleams. She uses a knee-high table as a vanity and a settee for visitors, and arranges her gospel tapes upright near its edge in alphabetical order: Shirley Caesar, James Cleveland, the Mississippi Mass Choir. Delia displays her favorite photographs, including one of a strikingly handsome black evangelist and snapshots of her godchildren, above a tin of cinnamon balls and chocolate candies she keeps for visitors.

Letters from relatives and former inmates she has bundled in a corner of her dresser. About two days a week, Delia receives visitors from the outside. On the morning of an appointment she will call one of her daughters down to her room to style her hair and paint and polish her fingernails and her toenails, if she plans to wear sandals.

At five-foot-seven, two hundred pounds plus, Delia's presence is hard to ignore. Impaired by her weight, which causes her blood pressure to soar and exacerbates her cellulitis, a condition marked by an inflammation beneath her skin, she has difficulty bending and often has to walk with a cane. Her problems are compounded by a long-time cigarette habit, a trait she despises. Often when exhaling a half-smoked generic, she'll pucker up her face, stub the cigarette out, and snap, "I hate these nasty little things."

One of Delia's most loyal daughters, Katie Molina, lives down the hall and makes it her business to check in on her "Ma" several times a day. She's serving a thirty-five-year sentence for murdering her husband with a crossbow. Restless and hardworking, she puts to use her care-giving skills and her passion for witchcraft and natural medicine by acting as Delia's personal nurse.

Sometimes when she wakes up in the morning, Delia finds a note with a happy face on it lying on her table, or maybe some flowers or herbs from the garden Katie and her companion, Lori, planted this spring behind the Fenwicks. She often scolds her "Ma" for eating too much junk food from commissary. Although staff and inmates often describe Katie's character as dubious, Delia needs help and often overlooks people's foibles if they show some goodness. On this rainy summer morning, she thinks a lot about Katie and Lori and how they give her hope.

The chills from her fever have settled deep into her bones, sending waves of hot and cold through her body. In a half-sleep, she watches through the boughs of the red cedar tree as the morning light grows stronger and the prison begins to stir. Reaching down with effort, Delia takes her cane and pounds on the wall to get the attention of Bonnie Foreshaw, her oldest friend in the cottage.

A tall, striking Jamaican woman with long dreadlocks that extend to the small of her back, Bonnie is serving the longest term in the prison—forty-five years for the murder of a pregnant woman. She is now working with a lawyer to get her case reopened in the hope of having her conviction reduced to manslaughter. Within seconds she throws her robe over her nightgown and runs to Delia's room. "My God, Miss D., what's wrong with you?" She takes an afghan from the bottom of the bed and wraps it snugly around her friend's shoulders.

"I'm cold, Bon, I'm so cold. Somethin's just not right."

By that time, other inmates, including Marie Rossignol, make their way to Delia's door. Marie's history at the Farm is legendary. Having weathered her "fallen woman" convictions in the '60s, drug addiction, and later the loss of her ten-year-old son to foster care, she probably knows the pitfalls of being incarcerated better than anyone. With an afghan thrown over her shoulders, she hobbles down the hall leaning on a cane. She takes one look at her friend of many years and shouts toward the CO's office, "There's gonna be a riot here if someone doesn't get her to the hospital soon."

Delia spends ten days in Lawrence & Memorial Hospital in New London. Flowers pour in by the dozens. She makes friends with the nurses and with a voluble white woman in the bed next to her, but avoids telling anyone where she lives—a detail inmates quickly learn to disguise. The hospital stay gives her time to think and to calm a growing anxiety. Within weeks, she is scheduled to go before the parole board, for the first time in seven years. And that entails reliving the one gaping wound in her life that will never heal. How she came to stab to death her twenty-one-year-old son and only child is something she often wants to think of as a dream she is sure to awake from. He had abused her and her common-law husband for years. But still, if only . . . Surely the parole board will excavate the memory like some phantom-filled ruin. Delia has carried those fears for weeks until they have broken her down and landed her flat in a hospital bed with the soap operas blasting and the white woman next to her talking nonstop about her grandchildren.

Once her fever breaks and her blood pressure stabilizes, Delia returns to her family at Sleepy Hollow. Two of her daughters have decorated her room with streamers and get-well cards, and Katie and Lori have posted a big sign on her door: *Welcome Back Miss D.*

Back in her bed now, she is surrounded by people who love her and know her goodness as she knows theirs. What counts most, she believes, is not what brings people here but how they prove themselves once inside. And the people she lives around and who have become her family are unlike most people she has ever met in her life outside.

"You won't find better people anywhere," Delia often tells her relatives and friends about the women in Fenwick South. "They may be lying to themselves about some things, but as far as being good-hearted and caring, I'd trust them with anything." She has faith that their love and support will carry her through to the parole hearing, and for that she thanks God every day. Because that is more than any one woman doing time at the Farm can ever hope for.

2

Niantic Love

Katie Molina will look you straight in the eye and tell you she didn't do it. She will tell you she bought the crossbow at a tag sale for her husband's birthday, but she would never shoot him with it. Why should she? They had an okay life, for God's sake. She will tell you that she was upstairs that night, getting her three young children ready for bed, when she heard noises downstairs. Rumbling noises, then loud, angry voices. Someone had broken into the house, she thought. She hustled the children and herself into the bathroom and locked the door. After a long silence she came out, crept to a phone and called the police. It wasn't until they arrived that she had the courage to go downstairs and investigate for herself. That's when she saw her husband lying dead on the couch, the arrow stuck through his chest—the arrow from the crossbow that she bought for his birthday.

Katie lives in Sleepy Hollow, a few doors down from Delia, whom she calls Ma. Here she sits, already having served nearly ten of the thirty-five years she received for a crime she swears she did not commit. Probably, she will tell you, because her husband worked for the Department of Correction and that worked against her.

Ten years. Katie repeats this in a whisper several more times before she lights another cigarette. She has exhausted all the education programs the prison has to offer. Received certificates in electronics, paralegal studies, veterinarian medicine and also worked in key-punch, where, she tells me, "I outworked everyone."

25

She does not want to wake her roommate Lori, asleep on the top bunk. Lori's father has just died and she is very depressed, and doesn't want to know anything. Katie and Lori, both in their mid-forties, have roomed together for six months. Katie used to have her own room, but gave it up to share a room with Lori. Everybody says they are lovers but they deny it.

"She's a big part of me," Katie says. She looks up at Lori all balled up under a mound of blankets. "We're more than friends and less than lovers. A CO could walk in our room at any time of day and would find us in separate beds."

Katie gives me a brief discourse on the gay hierarchy in Niantic. Some women pair off, others try to become studs, which entitles them to sleep around. Only about two percent of the women in Niantic are actually gay. Others just pretend they are until they leave and go back to their boyfriends or husbands. "Niantic love comes and goes," she says. "Most women just like to play house."

Katie sits in front of a painting of a wolf encircled by a medicine wheel given to them by a former inmate named Dakota. I admire its use of color and detail and ask if it holds any meaning. Katie mumbles something about wolves and their connection to the feminine spirit, then adds, as if to convey authority, "I'm half Indian."

Along the top edge of their wall, right below the ceiling, she's creating a mural that looks like an ancient cave painting. There's a deer and her fawn and some tigers and birds. She's not certain what it means yet, she's just compelled by the force of some spirit.

Lori wakes up, says nothing, then starts to work on her latest creation, a wheel of bird feathers she wants to hang on their wall. She collects materials from the lake shore and woods, things like feathers, twigs, leaves, and bark, then with yarn weaves them into beautiful tapestries. Katie takes one look at her and tells me Lori is feeling a lot better.

Lori was a professional chef once, Katie says, working mostly at expensive steak houses in Delaware. Ever since she was a child growing up on an asparagus farm in Maryland, food has been her passion. Lori trained by working five years in a kosher catering house. She has learned how to make ice carvings and work banquets. She has done short-order cooking and served seven hundred meals a night. She once had her own deli in a Hispanic neighborhood in Wilmington where she served a ninety-nine-cent breakfast.

"That was my gimmick to get them to come back for lunch," pipes

Lori, at last. She continues on her own, explaining that then she started doing drugs, went out of control, and ended up committing robberies in New York and Connecticut. She served her New York sentence at Riker's Island, where her leg was badly damaged during a riot. Trying to get out of the way of a guard, she got struck several times with a nightstick by another guard. She cannot talk about it without crying. It's left her with a deep distrust and paranoia when it comes to authority.

She looks at me for the first time this morning and says, "When I first met you I thought you were an informant."

Naturally, the hardest part of prison life for Lori is the food. As vegetarians, Lori and Katie rarely eat prison meals, except to take vegetables and fruit off their trays so they can put them on the cereal or soups they get from commissary. To supplement their diet they've put in a garden behind Fenwick South filled with tomato, basil, oregano, and chive plants. They make fresh bouquets out of the herbs and pass them around to inmates and staff. Katie uses the herbs in teas, as part of her religion, which is a combination of Eastern mysticism, witchcraft, and Native American spiritualism.

Some inmates in Sleepy Hollow call Katie and Lori eccentric, saying their diet is a disguised form of an eating disorder. Both women are anemically pale and bone thin. Some of the women say Katie drinks regular doses of Milk of Magnesia, then spends too much time in the bathroom purging.

No matter, most of the inmates are amazed at how well the two women get along. Unlike another "couple" in the cottage whose relationship mirrors the abusive behaviors most inmates would like to forget, Katie and Lori never raise their voices to one other, and always show respect. Katie's in-your-face intensity blends well with Lori's mild-mannered reserve. They never take each other for granted. Whenever Katie compliments her, Lori blushes like a schoolgirl and says, "Ah, now stop it."

Every morning Katie and Lori feed the raccoons and stray cats in a patch of woods across from their cottage. The seagulls, too, always know when the women are coming. Lori walks out with a bag filled with bread crumbs, cups her hands around her mouth, and lets out loud "Tuuuu-Weeeps! Tuuuu-Weeeps!" that sound just like the birds. From every direction, they soar and fold in around her, like a wide lace veil about to scoop her up and carry her away.

Lori wears her jeans down below her waist, urban guerrilla style.

She doesn't do this for show, there's no pretense about her. It's just that she's lost about sixty pounds of the two hundred she carried when she arrived at jail, thanks mostly to Katie.

They met through a mentor program, which matched older inmates like Katie with the younger inmates of Fenwick North. Even though Lori was older, her status as a first offender made her eligible for Fenwick North. Suffering leg and back pains from injuries inflicted at Riker's Island and from other illnesses, she welcomed Katie's caretaking nature. Within a few weeks, the two became inseparable.

However, there was one major problem. Katie had remarried. About three years after she was sentenced and settled in, according to inmates and staff, she started up a love affair with the electronics instructor at the prison school. Word got out, as it inevitably does in such a cloistered environment, and the instructor was fired. Nevertheless, the two carried on through letters, phone calls, and weekly visits. Eventually the couple got married in a ceremony at the Niantic prison chapel. Until he found out about Lori, Katie's husband supplied her with clothes, money, and just about anything she needed that was legal. He brought in his children to visit her on the weekends, and by all appearances they seemed a happy family.

Not surprisingly, when Katie's husband got word through the prison grapevine that his wife was involved with a woman, her marriage dissolved. By then, Katie and Lori were receiving a steady income from Lori's father, so the split wasn't catastrophic financially. Through correspondence, Katie convinced Lori's father that through the use of herbs and Oriental medicine she could cure his daughter of whatever ailed her. After a few months, Lori started feeling much stronger. She says she owes it all to Katie.

When it comes to Katie's modus operandi, correction officers and inmates say she is a smooth operator. According to at least one CO, even before Lori came into the picture, Katie had abused her role as mentor by messing around with one too many of the young women in Fenwick North. The guards and some inmates likened her to a spiderwoman who preys on the vulnerable to get whatever she needs. They say Lori's poor health and shy nature made her Katie's perfect prey.

Given Katie's history of sexual misconduct, it is difficult to see how officials allowed the two women to room together. Nevertheless, cohabitation in Niantic is by no means rare. Some COs bend the rules, I am told, to keep peace in a cottage. Otherwise it is hard on the roommate who is not part of the couple and usually has to leave when the girlfriend shows up.

Regardless of her faults, Katie has redeemed herself somewhat by working hard and acting as the cottage's medicine woman. She brings inmates herbal remedies from her garden, mixing a potion to use as aromatherapy, or she prescribes a diet of vegetables and juices to bring them back to mental and physical health. When an older inmate gets word that a relative is sick or has died, Katie dutifully rushes to her side and performs Shiatsu or some other massage technique. Once I walked into the foyer of Fenwick South and found Katie standing over and massaging the neck of an inmate who had just found out that a young relative had died a violent death. As the woman wailed and shook, Katie's movements rocked with her.

Katie's number one patient is Delia. After she had returned from the hospital that summer, Katie and Lori watched over her like a pair of labradors, making sure she ate right and got her sleep. Each morning they check in on her, making certain her blue plastic cup is filled with ice water and the straw basket that sits on her in table is brimming with crackers. They help her dress by putting on her stockings or zipping up her dress, and often massage her swollen feet. Once when Delia went on furlough to a big family reunion, Lori made her birthday cards to give to relatives. At Christmas, she made her a Santa Claus out of a plastic honey bear bottle. Another time, she made Delia a money box out of a coffee can with the words "feed me" written across the front. Delia took it to a family reunion and dinner dance in Boston, where she placed it next to her. By the end of the evening she had collected about seventy-five dollars. She used the money to buy a new outfit to wear to her parole hearing.

"We love that woman," Lori says. "Miss D. is about the only other person in this place that I get emotional about."

Katie and Lori have become Sleepy Hollow's custodians. They wash the floors, clean the bathrooms, keep the front steps clean, and have planted containers of geraniums on the porches, making the cottage stand out from all the others. They collect the laundry and clean the staff office. They make about $1.40 a day. While COs appreciate the hard work and nice touches, some inmates complain that the two women manipulate jobs away from other inmates, and curry too much favor with COs.

But Katie and Lori seem to ignore the criticism, and like clockwork, buzz through the hallways every morning tidying, cleaning, and restocking the supply closets. They have other interests as well.

Early one crisp morning, Katie and Lori sit in their room nursing a baby mourning dove that has fallen from its nest. They often keep wounded animals in their room; some COs know about it, but have never said anything. Katie keeps the bird in a box padded with tissue. She has also placed a hand mirror on the floor with some bird seed in a plastic lid in front of it. "We don't know if it's a boy or a girl," Katie says. She chews on a saltine cracker, then picks up the bird and cradles it in her hand. She sticks out her tongue and lets the bird nibble and peck at the masticated cracker. Lori winks. "You can sure tell who the mama is," she says.

Lori is sitting on the lower bunk making a mural for the crows with sticks, string, and mica she has collected. She will hang it outside her window when she is through. She glues the mica and string together with the sap from a pine cone. She and Katie have read in a book that crows like to put mirrors in their nests, so they're hoping the birds will take the mica. "The crows yell at us every morning," Lori says. "They know which window is ours." Katie places the mourning dove on the floor and watches it walk back and forth in front of the mirror. She coos and makes kissing noises to it. "You might think this is a wildlife refuge," Katie says. "But actually they kind of rescue us."

Katie starts to think about dinner. She does all the cooking. In the winter she makes apple pies, then bakes them on top of her radiator. Tonight though, she's thinking about pasta primavera. They cannot have hot plates in their rooms, but she will take the vegetables from the garden, soak them in hot water from the tap, add some instant noodles, then top it off with herbs and some processed cheese she bought from commissary. They might ask their friend Robyn who lives upstairs to dinner. She is a vegetarian too.

Katie and Lori rarely allow anyone in their room. They consider it a holy place, their sanctuary. Nor do they encourage relatives and friends to visit them at the Visitors' Center. "Who wants somebody to come here and complain about all their problems?" Katie says. "They just bum you out. Then you have to turn around and go back and face all the stress in here."

But even before she can start thinking about dinner, there is so much other work to be done. The garden needs constant attention.

She and Lori are writing and illustrating two children's books. She is writing a book of poetry and has just finished weaving a throw rug from thirty skeins of yarn. "We never have enough time," Katie says, as she cleans up the mess the mourning dove has just made. "The only way to survive this place is to keep busy, busy, busy."

3

Candyland

If the lifestyle in Fenwick South evokes melodies from a lite-fm radio station, then Fenwick North pulsates with the improvisational rhythms of jazz fusion. Before I visit their neighbor next door, Delia and Katie tell me it is like entering another galaxy. They're right on.

The unit is buzzing with brassy, street-smart women in their late teens and twenties, most of them experiencing the odyssey of confinement for the first time. Known as Candyland by the older inmates, its culture demands sharp survival skills and a quick eye for the ever-shifting hierarchy. Most of these young offenders anchor themselves by finding a lover or joining a gang. Prostitution and drugs lead the list of convictions, followed by larceny and assault. For the most part, sentences are short, ranging from three months to two years.

It's the Fourth of July. I've been invited to room 14 on the second floor of Fenwick North, where Gina and Sheila are lounging on their bunk beds swapping stories about life on the streets. Both were sentenced on prostitution and drug convictions; it is their first time at the Farm. Though they have grown up in vastly different social circles, as streetwalkers they have a sure-fire bond.

"I'd pick up any guy and give him head for twenty dollars, just so I could buy some more crack," Gina says, popping a fireball candy into her mouth. "One guy paid me $150 to pee in front of him."

Sheila pulls out a cigarette and plugs it into her mouth. She smirks and says, "Well, I had this one guy who wanted me to pee on his face for fifty bucks but nothin' would come out."

The women look at each other and laugh. Then Gina props her pillow against the window sill and gives a languid sigh. "All those guys out there are so obsessed with their fantasies. I mean, what you have to do to get money off them is pretty disgusting and humiliating."

Gina traces her finger along the springs of the upper bunk, her auburn hair falling in soft curls along her pillow, her porcelain skin marred by red lesions. She comes from an upper-middle-class New Haven family. "Before I started doing crack I was a straight-A student. Never did anything wrong. Then one night I was at a friend's house and I took one hit and I was gone. Next thing I know I'm out on the streets givin' head."

Unlike the sublimity of Sleepy Hollow, the constant turnover and age level gives Candyland an atmosphere of chaos and suspicion. Doors slam, televisions thunder, and the word "fuck," used emphatically for nearly every part of speech, echoes through the halls. The corridors exude a time-worn gloom, yellow stretches of smoke-stained walls stenciled with faded flowers by former inmates. The compact rooms consist of bunk beds, two dressers, and a wardrobe. Photos, toiletries, cardboard ashtrays, and not much else give most of the cubicles an air of transiency. Inmates come and go in turnstile fashion, barely leaving their mark.

Before she got arrested for prostitution, Gina was living with Ed, a former intravenous drug-user, in a dilapidated neighborhood of New Haven. Each morning around 11 A.M. she strolled down Ferry Street, sometimes in a short skirt with high heels, sometimes just wearing jeans and a sweat shirt. Twelve hours later she returned home, strung out on crack. Ed would be lying upright in bed waiting. He often begged her to stop doing drugs and sleeping around with other men. But Ed, a burly man with a patient heart, also told her not to worry, he would always stand by her.

Gina pops another fireball candy into her mouth and tosses the wrapper, missing the trash can. She tosses another wrapped candy into the air and it lands in my lap. "Every time he said that, man, I'd freak. I'd do anything to get him to throw me out so I'd have an excuse to go right back out on the streets."

The blotches on her ankles and calves came from popping too much dope. "I have staph infections, leukemia, and diabetes, too," she tells us. Sheila sits with her arms wrapped around her bony frame listening to Gina's compulsive talk. "Man, that's a fuckin' drag," she says.

Sheila and Gina met only a few weeks before, when they first came to the Farm. Within no time they discovered a mutual love of rich foods, a desire amplified by the starchy and bland prison diet, which many inmates dress up with chili sauce bought from commissary.

To placate her cravings, Gina has pasted above her bed magazine photos of chocolate ganaches, prime ribs, cherry pies, and butterscotch praline ice cream. She tells food stories about restaurants she has been to, her favorite Italian pastry shops, and which delis stock the best bagels. "It, like, keeps me sane," she says.

As street dwellers, the women detest the prison rules. The doors to their rooms are locked from 11:30 P.M. to 6:30 A.M. If they need to go to the bathroom, they have to slide a piece of cardboard under their door to signal the CO on duty. Gina says that the week before, she waited forty-five minutes before a CO showed up to unlock the door. Some inmates raise a ruckus instead by pounding on the door and shouting, waking others up. COs often respond by giving the inmate a discipline called a "six o'clock," which confines her to her room for twelve hours beginning at 6 P.M. "It really sucks," Sheila says.

Candy, who lives three doors down with her cousin Michelle, comes in and sits on the lower bunk next to Gina. Both women are in on drug charges. Candy also worked as a prostitute. She holds in her hand a certificate she earned for completing a drug awareness program and a laminated card with the Serenity Prayer on it. She has large green eyes, tight blond Shirley Temple curls, and dimples.

"It's a good program because it gets into your past and how you got here," she tells me, coyly. Candy says she grew up in Waterbury and has never known her father. Her mother was a drug addict and her stepfather raped her from the time she was five until she was eleven. At thirteen, she says, she started prostituting so she could buy drugs for herself and her boyfriend. She's never learned to read and can barely write. She's memorized the Serenity Prayer and recites it to herself every morning and night.

"When I get out of here I'm going to be a drug counselor," she says, twisting her curls with her index finger.

"That's cool," Sheila says.

Because of the high percentage of women serving time at the

Farm on drug charges, the prison offers dozens of programs to help inmates overcome their addictions and revamp their self-esteem. Candy has graduated from a six-week course for young offenders run by counselors from the addiction services office. Following on the twelve-step, addiction-as-a-disease philosophy, counselors lead participants through the wreckage of their young lives, allowing them to talk about how the addiction problems of their parents or siblings have affected their lives. For women with little education, the programs give them the first opportunity to talk about such issues.

At noon, COs Benjamin Cuevas and Susan Bollenbech walk through the halls announcing that the barbecue for the Fourth of July picnic has started. "I can't stomach that crap," Gina says, turning to Sheila. "Just bring me back some ice cream."

Sheila, Candy, and Michelle dash through the hall and down a back stairway that leads to a fenced recreation yard. Across the street, Bride Lake sparkles under the mid-summer sun and a cool breeze breaks through the thick air. The old brick school house sits across the street a few hundred feet from the prison chapel. Gathered in the yard, the women sit on picnic tables next to a clothesline and a volleyball net. Others find a sunny spot on the ground. They fill their paper plates with burgers, potato chips, coleslaw, and watermelon, and talk about how it's the first decent meal they have had since they arrived. Sitting cross-legged atop one picnic table, a woman with the word "love" tattooed on her upper arm tells the story about how she had been framed and unjustly sent to jail. "On the very night I'm bartending, someone hid an ounce of cocaine behind the bar and I get busted," she says. "My boss wouldn't testify for me, nothin'."

Similar stories from other inmates flow forth. Then someone brings up the subject of prison food.

"This isn't meat, it's soy protein," one woman yells. "Hell, I wouldn't feed this to my dog."

"The food here's great if you've got chronic diarrhea," says another woman in her early thirties, who sports a thin mustache. " I've been plugged up since I got here."

Officer Cuevas leans up against the wall letting the banter fly before he says, "This isn't a Holiday Inn, you know. If you didn't do the crime, you wouldn't have to serve the time."

"Amen," says one African American woman whose talk is peppered with the name of Jesus.

"This place is worse than Hell," shouts an impish blond-haired woman with few teeth.

Sheila sits with Candy and Michelle, chewing on her last bite of hot dog and picking seeds out of her watermelon. "You got that all wrong," she shouts. "Clean sheets, three meals a day, hot water. Compared to living on the streets this place is a resort."

She turns back to her conversation with Michelle. They've been comparing notes on their relationships with men. Whenever Michelle's boyfriend hit her she always hit him back. Finally she stabbed him and ended up in prison. She's hopeful, though. He's now taking care of their daughter and attending an Angry Men's group, to learn how to control his temper.

Sheila leans back against the brick wall, blows smoke rings into the air, and takes in all the action. After a few seconds she gives Michelle a wary grin and says, "Yeah, that's what they all say. But the real truth is, once they hit you, they hit you forever. Last guy who told me he'd stop, put me into the hospital with a concussion a week later."

While the women relax and eat vanilla ice cream, Imiga, a thirty-seven-year-old Korean woman, zigzags through the yard picking up plates, forks, and cups, and tossing them into a large metal trash can. She works on fast-forward, talking in a clipped English that few inmates and staff can understand. Solid, sleek, and muscular, she stands out in her black Spandex biking shorts, metallic blue halter top, and pink headband.

She has worked her way up from Tennessee to Connecticut by dancing in topless bars. Soon after she arrived, she and her eighth husband were arrested for selling drugs. At the Farm she works in the kitchen and takes great pride in the job. Any negative criticism about the food cuts through her pride, and she's quick to react. After overhearing one inmate at the picnic complain about finding a hair in her mashed potatoes the week before, Imiga comes to a halt and stammers, "God damn, I work hard in the kitchen and there is no hair. I keep things clean." She whirls around and continues packing the rest of the supplies. "I got a lot of problems already and these people only giving me more," she mutters over and over.

Gina sits on her bunk and watches the whole scene from her

second-story window. "Hey Sheila! Don't forget my ice cream!" she yells down. Minutes later as I walk through the empty hallway toward the front entrance, I find Gina sitting on the stairs waiting for me. "I gotta tell you something," she whispers, then looks around for eavesdroppers. There is no one in sight. "You want to talk to someone in this shithole who has AIDS?"

We go back to her room and close the door. She rolls back on her bunk. "I hardly go out of my room because I'm afraid of picking up germs," she says, barely above a whisper. "I tested positive before I came in here." While she enjoys Sheila's company, Gina says she keeps everything to herself because she feels she'll be "dissed" and shunned. She uses the leukemia and diabetes story to explain her blemishes and frequent staph infections, but has told no one except the prison counselors about having the dreaded virus. Not even Sheila knows. Despite their camaraderie as prostitutes, the stigma of AIDS as a mysterious, deadly plague still prevails. If an inmate has it, she likely hides it. A lawsuit brought by the Connecticut Civil Liberties Union and settled in 1988 guarantees inmate confidentiality in these matters. Consequently no one, not even many of the staff, knows who carries the virus. Though the medical clinic tests inmates routinely for syphilis, gonorrhea, and other venereal diseases, AIDS tests are voluntary.

Gina talks some more about being tormented by germs. "Anything could lower my resistance," she says. "I could pick up athlete's foot in a shower stall or in the hallways. And they only change the sheets around here once a week and I'm freaked, because I'm sleeping on all this bacteria."

Her T-cell count has fallen below four hundred and each day in prison she worries about it dropping even more. She picked up the virus from her boyfriend, Ed, who ran support workshops on the subject. There wasn't much to their love life, she says. They stopped having sex because they were passing the virus back and forth, wreaking havoc on each other's immune systems.

In her drawer Gina keeps a stack of letters tied up with a ponytail holder. Most come from older johns who are obsessed with trying to reform her. One man, fifty-one years old, comes to visit her every Saturday and tells her that it doesn't matter if she has the virus, he will always take care of her. Another, a wealthy New Haven business man named Robert, who is also a friend of her family's, consoles her and promises to help her when she is released from prison. Gina accepts all the attention with a coy nonchalance.

"It's nice that they like me and everything," she says, as the chatter from the picnic below her window subsides. "But I still love Ed."

As I came to learn, for every prostitute in Niantic there is likely to be a sugar daddy in waiting. Well into middle age and sometimes way beyond, these fellows supply money and security, and often fill in as the woman's only family. Many try to reform their objects of desire with pleading letters or phone calls. The women, in turn, play along to get more goods. Though they often make fun of or chide their benefactors, at the same time the women boast of the clothes and cars they received before coming to jail and of the man's ongoing attentiveness. The partnership is indeed symbiotic. As long as she feeds into his delusions or fantasies, the cash and the "love" keep coming.

Gina shifts from talking about the men in her life and returns to the topic of AIDS in prison. She is fidgety and starts to chew on a fingernail. "People in here are so stupid about this disease. They think they have so much to fear from me, and the thing is they can hurt me so much more than I can hurt them. I have nightmares of dying in this place." Before she can say anymore, Sheila bursts through the door holding a cup of vanilla ice cream. Gina gives me a nervous glance and our conversation comes to an abrupt end.

The next week, Candy, a recent graduate of the prison's drug awareness program, is sent to segregation for returning from a furlough with a "dirty" urine specimen. One morning that same week during breakfast, Imiga is serving breakfast trays when an inmate comments that "the food sucks." So provoked, Imiga slams down the pack of trays, picks up a chair, and hurls it across the room, just missing the inmate's head. The guards immediately usher her to segregation where, in her obsessive fashion, she spends the next fifteen days scrubbing floors and washing walls.

"I got a lot of problems already and these people only giving me more," she mutters over and over the next time I see her.

In Candyland, the inhabitants change from week to week. By early fall, Gina and Sheila return home, as do Candy and Michelle. Imiga stays until the following summer, engaging in a flurry of activity until the last moment. What happens to the women once they leave is often a mystery. Many return to their hometowns, only to get swallowed up in the nearest urban underworld. They rarely write, and they make themselves hard to trace, unless an inmate spots them on the streets. Many eventually land back at the Farm.

Stephanie, fifteen, came to Candyland a month after Gina and Sheila left. She stabbed a john, a fifty-five-year-old man, and had begun serving a five-year sentence. Dark-skinned with large brown eyes, she has an anxiety-ridden look caused by her fear of being assaulted by an inmate.

Before being sent to Candyland, Stephanie was put into a holding cell at ADM, a small room with phones. Officials photographed her for an identification card and told her about the procedures and policies of the prison. Stephanie was then strip-searched for drugs and contraband, doused for lice and crabs, given a pap test, basic blood work, a urinalysis for drugs, and a basic physical. In the medical unit, counselors told her about prison programs for inmates with substance-abuse problems and gave her a brief lecture on how AIDS is transmitted. Before being assigned to housing, all inmates go through the same procedures.

Stephanie is classified as a maximum-security risk, which means she will be handcuffed and shackled every time she leaves her cottage. She is sent to live in Candyland with forty-two other inmates. CO Bollenbech, whose pale blue eyes exude a protectiveness inmates warm to, sits the teen-ager down and gives her a litany of do's and don't's. "Everybody must be up at 7:15 for breakfast, then dressed by 9 A.M. You clean your own food tray. No smoking in bed. Keep your radio down. You're allowed to make collect calls only. If you need a Kotex or a tampon they're in the front office along with the curling irons. First and second floor inmates don't mix."

Stephanie picks up the plastic bag stuffed with her clothes and lumbers up the stairs. She keeps her eyes focused on the floor. At the top of the landing, an African American woman in her thirties gives Stephanie the once-over. The teenager flinches. "My biggest fear is that some bitch will force me to become gay," she whispers. "She'll sneak into my room some night and there won't be nothin' I can do about it."

4

A Warden's Legacy

Behind the Fenwicks, next to the old greenhouses rests a thirty-foot square plot hemmed in by a white picket fence lined with pansies. On a late August morning, the Farm's new garden abounds with shapely summer squashes, plump red tomatoes and herbs and greens. Under a cloudless sky, inmates in cotton shorts and T-shirts smudged with dirt, hoe, weed, or carry armfuls of vegetables into the greenhouse across the road. Volunteers from the local garden club have worked with the women since early spring, teaching them how to fertilize the soil, determine the sunlight needs of each vegetable, and design, plant, and care for the garden. The scene perhaps resembles those of fifty years before, when Niantic was a working farm. If anything, today's small garden symbolizes a rekindling of the earlier philosophy, which trumpeted the idea that inmate idleness could be redirected and that values would be instilled by hard, constructive work.

Inside the greenhouse, Betty, an inmate from Jamaica, stands over an electric skillet, stir-frying a mound of diced squash. She smiles as she warbles softly a gospel song, giving the atmosphere an inviting glow. One of the recreation supervisors brings in zucchini bread made from the squash she had taken home the night before. The bread, along with a bowl of fresh strawberries and blueberries, paper plates, and plastic forks, are laid out under the greenhouse's glass canopy on a long wooden table decorated with marigolds.

Before long, the inmates stow their garden tools and assemble near the food. Betty passes plates of her stir-fried squash to two Puerto Rican women who reluctantly accept the dish. "This looks weird," one of the women says with a scowl. But after savoring its spicy, warm flavors, she asks for seconds. Throughout the harvest lunch, the inmates share stories about gardens in their lives: one tended by a neighbor in a housing project; another by a grandfather; and some they'd seen in magazines. Now they can talk about their own garden and how amazing it is that the food on their plates had sprouted from what were mere seeds months before.

As Betty spoons up seconds and thirds of her squash she extols, "This is the way life should always be."

In Warden Carol Dunn's own vernacular, the garden project's real aim is "to teach women to recreate without using alcohol or drugs." Getting women out of the crowded cottages, and away from the blare of television soap operas, might at least ease tensions, particularly for long-term inmates.

Appointed warden earlier that spring, Dunn has added the garden project to the long roster of behavioral reform programs. Several years before, she had worked as a counselor at the Farm, and many of the older inmates who knew her then liked her and were pleased to see her return. Her style is personal but no-nonsense. Inmates and staff describe her as savvy, sweet-tempered, and fair. She answers inmate requests by sending personal notes or by visiting their cottages. Inmates tell me they can voice their concerns to her without feeling intimidated.

Soon after she began her new job, I interviewed her over the telephone about her goals for the prison. Her voice had a girlish quality, edged with a hardness which I suspected came from being around jails for most of her adult life. When I met with her to discuss this book project, I was surprised to find her somewhat older than I had expected.

Her office is on the first floor of ADM, down the hall from the nucleus of the prison's operations. Perpetually clogged with activity, the place reverberates with the discordant scratching of two-way radios and the grating buzz of an alarm that sounds each time the front door opens. The long galley contains the telephone switchboard and the communications center where COs receive and relay messages and record the prison's "count" five to seven times a day. It also serves as the entrance and exit point for inmates.

In contrast, Dunn's office has a quiet appeal. Painted in pale blue and pink, it evokes a country femininity. Straw hats with pink silk ribbons drape one wall and on another are displayed Dunn's prize winning photographs—Mediterranean scenes of cobblestoned alleys and ornate doorways. An antique Rembrandt camera, once used to photograph inmates, rests on a tripod near a window.

An attractive woman with an athletic build, Dunn speaks with a polished candidness, occasionally peppering her sentences with four-letter words. She has worked in the system for nearly twenty years and it is a vital part of her identity. Unlike wardens from earlier decades, Dunn says she has no romantic notions about her position. She has been around long enough to know that it will take much more than a prison term and a few encounter groups to set most inmates' lives on track. More and more, prisons of the 1990s are as concerned with rehabilitating drug addicts as they are with reforming criminal behavior, given that some 85 percent of sentences are drug related, according to Dunn.

In our first interviews Dunn carries herself with an official stiffness, but she gradually gives me glimpses of a more relaxed nature, someone who might even enliven a dull party. She is nervous about her new position, she tells me. Considering that she will be eligible for retirement in the next few years, Niantic may well be her swan song. She is eager to leave a legacy.

One of her main aims is to open the first residential drug-treatment center in the correction system. Her biggest supporter is her boss, Larry R. Meachum, Connecticut's Commissioner of Correction. Blond, granite-jawed, and erect, he looks like the central casting image of a prison guard, but with a twist. At a time when policymakers doubt the effectiveness of rehabilitation and are calling for paramilitary boot camps as an alternative, Meachum stands out as an old-fashioned do-gooder. His philosophy has become the center of a debate over where the state's beleaguered prison system—with around 12,000 inmates—goes from here. Though some are inspired by his philosophy of controlling inmates while allowing them some personal freedom, others say he embodies everything that is wrong with the criminal justice system.

The union representing prison guards publicly criticizes Meachum, saying he allows too much movement of inmates, which has resulted in more assaults on guards. Citizen groups say the system's

$1 billion capital-spending plan set in motion in the mid-'80s and aimed to double the number of prison cells by 1995, is tainting their communities and making them unsafe. But over and over, Meachum stands by his conviction that positive reinforcement and positive environments equal good prison management. The more you clamp down in an overcrowded situation, he tells reporters whenever the prison system is targeted, the more likely it is to explode.

Like the omnipresent crucifix hanging in the Catholic parish house, Meachum's framed photograph emblazons the walls of many Niantic offices. Even so, many staff are not overly reverent when discussing the man and his policies. The guards often make flippant remarks about him, saying he likes inmates better than his own staff.

Dunn acknowledges the criticism but genuinely seems to like Meachum and his efforts to keep the prisons humane. Another item on the commissioner's agenda is to make the system smoke-free, a measure the warden also embraces. As a former smoker herself, she talks about the possibility almost evangelically. When I open the pack of matches she hands me, I find a row of toothpicks instead, announcing an annual "smoke-out." "You can keep them," she says.

Dunn is also determined to create a wellness program for her staff. The inherent stress and constant flux of working as a prison guard can easily seep into and destroy one's personal life. It can be a crazy, surreal kind of existence. "We smoke too much, we drink too much, and we mess around too much," Dunn says, using the first person plural only for emphasis. "We need help too."

The notion of retiring in the next few years, at which time she will be in her early forties makes her anxious. She has spent most of her adult life in the corrections system. To leave, regardless of the generous pension package, and return to the slow spin of a job on the outside, will be a tough adjustment. She has worked her way through the ranks and served previously as a warden for the Brooklyn Correctional Center, a medium-security prison near Hartford. She wonders if she can ever top such accomplishments in another field.

"I can't imagine not having 'warden' to fall back on," she says. "That would be hard to take."

She pauses and offers a few glimpses of her private life—a new home upstate, her desire to write photo essays at some point, her fondness for her niece and nephew, and her love of traveling.

Dunn first came to Niantic in 1974, as part of an internship program through the University of Connecticut. She was twenty-two years old and very green. On her first day, she was handed a wad of keys and told to take twenty-seven inmates down to the lake to go fishing. "I couldn't believe it," she'd tell me in a later interview. "Here I was sent out into the woods with these twenty-seven women, and I didn't know if they were all going to jump me or what."

As she sat on a picnic table supervising the activity, inmates started chatting with her. "This one inmate asked me if I was going to apply for a job at this place, and I said 'no' and she said 'why not' and I said, 'Because this place is fucked up,' " Dunn said, referring to the overall ambience of prison culture.

"That's why you should come here," the inmate told her.

Later that summer she was working as a waitress at a Lums restaurant when she received a call from Warden Janet York who asked her to come work at Niantic. "I looked around at all these people in this restaurant and thought to myself, 'get me out of here.' I immediately said 'yes.' "

She worked as a CO and then as a counselor at Niantic for a total of eleven years before transferring to one of the men's prisons. In 1989 she was promoted to warden and served first at a minimum-security jail near Hartford that held inmates mostly convicted on DWI charges. Two years later she was appointed the warden at Brooklyn, where she expanded drug- and alcohol-treatment programs. In 1991, Commissioner Meachum gave the facility a rating of "excellent."

Dunn liked the pace and intensity of working in a men's prison, and accepted with reluctance the offer to head the women's prison at Niantic. People in the system still refer cynically to it as a country club with a rather somnolent lifestyle. Most people drawn to corrections, including Dunn to some extent, thrive on the roller coaster unpredictability more likely to be found in a men's prison.

Yet the myth of Niantic as a pastoral farm was fading long before she arrived. Though still not as frequent as at men's prisons, assaults, drug trafficking, and gang activity had spiraled. Though they had yet to find guns and other weapons, officials were confiscating more makeshift contraband, like toothbrushes with razor blades fastened between the bristles.

Like most who have been in the system for some years, Dunn

believes the new women's prison being constructed only a few hundred yards from where she sits is merely a catch basin for the growing number of women being sent to jail. Designed to hold some 350 medium- and maximum-security inmates and scheduled to open in 1994, Dunn and other staff say it will fill to overflowing in no time.

"Perhaps if they stopped building prisons and started concentrating on poor families in the inner city, maybe there'd be more opportunity for change," Dunn says.

Though pressured by correction officials in Hartford to become the first warden of the $55 million complex, if she decides not to retire, Dunn prefers staying in her present job. Ideally, the original farm may eventually revert to a minimum-security prison similar to the prison's earlier days. That idea appeals to her.

Like Gilchrist and others who have worked here for years, Dunn talks wistfully about the days before the deluge when it was plausible to think you could change lives. She aims to recapture at least a slice of those days.

The story of Niantic is full of high hopes, dashed promises, and episodes of steady progress. Because of its status as one of the first and most progressive women's reformatories in the country, staff to this day often sound like torchbearers. Yet conditions in Niantic in the early 1990s stand in stark contrast to the late teens when the State Farm for Women first opened its doors to twenty-nine "troublesome, diseased and defective women who for years had been clogging the courts and filling the jails," according to an annual report from 1918. The occupations of those first inmates ranged from a spinner in a cotton mill to a wrestler in a carnival.

Up until the mid-1800s, women offenders across the country were typically housed in cell blocks inside men's prisons. Some states later built custodial units away from the prison. Supervised by a matron, they were equipped with sewing machines or wash tubs where the women worked.

The momentum for establishing separate reformatories for women stemmed, in part, from the rise of the Progressive movement in the mid-1800s to the early 1900s, which sought to implement political, business, and social reforms. The movement generated a number of antivice campaigns, in which civic groups, religious and temperance organizations, and feminists joined forces to cleanse society of the "social evil" and its likely consequence, venereal disease.

By the end of the century, prostitution, like liquor, was being targeted as one of society's most dangerous internal enemies. Pressured
by reformers, cities closed down their red-light or vice districts in the
early 1900s, and the prostitutes who inhabited them scattered. But
instead of ridding the streets of sexual indecency, as reformers had
hoped, shutting down the districts drove the women underground,
and prostitution became more closely linked with liquor, drugs,
theft, and violence.

With the advent of World War I and the alarm over the rise of
venereal diseases and the so-called camp followers of the national
guard camps who appeared to be spreading them, the campaigns
against prostitution continued. For decades, prison reformers, particularly in the Northeast, had used the antivice soapbox to gather
support for women's reformatories, arguing that by sequestering
fallen women in rural prisons, they would shield society from those
who spread disease. In addition, the reformatories would "rescue"
not only prostitutes but also women of a wayward nature who might
be reclaimed. Laws of the period also took aim at the sentiments
toward "deviant" women, making it possible to incarcerate violators
for minor offenses involving immoral conduct. Ultimately, the reformatories reflected the society's view of what constituted true
womanhood.

In Connecticut, it was the militant, all-female Committee on De-
linquent Women of the Connecticut Prison Association that pressured politicians to take action. The legislature eventually granted
$50,000 to buy a 750-acre tract called Bride Lake Farm. Formerly an
Indian hunting ground, the property was later parceled into three
farms. The bucolic setting contained the lake and state preserve
stocked with California salmon and trout. Four farm houses with
barns and outbuildings served as the first cottages, which were renovated as sleeping quarters, a sewing room, a nursery, and a medical
unit. To accomplish the goal of reforming the women, officials set
out to make the tract a self-sufficient working farm.

As altruistic as the reformatories seemed, prison historians like
Nicole Hahn Rafter point out that they also became instruments of
differential justice that punished women more harshly than men for
sexual activity. In the early days, Niantic's inmate profile reflected
those inequities. Most of the women serving time had violated laws
targeting immoral sexual behavior, such as lascivious carriage, adul-
tery, prostitution, being a "wayward woman" and showing a "man-

ifest danger of falling into habits of vice." Men were rarely sentenced for similar offenses.

At the same time, reformers had accomplished their main goal of establishing prisons designed architecturally and philosophically for women, a process that took Connecticut nearly sixty years. A year after Niantic opened, prison officials announced in an annual report the great progress they had made and how they could look to the future with pride: "Outdoors the women have carried water, chopped wood, mowed the yards, cared for the roads and paths, weeded, dug potatoes, gathered and prepared vegetables, picked and canned blueberries, cared for pigs and last, but not least, cut ten acres of ensilage, helped in loading it into the carts, assisted in feeding the cutter, tramped it into the silo, and are now planning to husk three hundred bushels of field corn." A few years later another report proclaimed: "The work helps to build bodies and to strengthen high-strung nervous creatures that come to us worn out by their habits of late hours, improper eating and vile indulgence."

As was common at most other reformatories, treating venereal diseases became the prison's primary focus, and in the first several years, medical personnel reported about five cases a week. Every woman admitted to the Farm was examined by a nurse, who ran blood and other tests on the inmate, which were sent to a state medical laboratory for examination. If the reports came back positive for gonorrhea or if the patient showed clinical symptoms of the disease, she received daily applications of a solution of argyrol, potassium permanganate, silver nitrate, or iodine. The process was repeated until the inmate received a negative test or her symptoms disappeared.

The Wassermann test for syphilis was also administered. If positive, women were given six injections of neoarsphenamine, an arsenic derivative, "at the rate of one a week, with an intramuscular injection of mercury or gray oil given mid-week," according to an annual report. The treatment was applied up to three to four times, with rest intervals in between. The prison required an infected inmate to have three negative tests each for gonorrhea and syphilis before she would be considered for parole. To supplement the injections, the women were also given medicinal baths in metal tubs. In the first two years the prison was open, officials took 438 tests, mostly for syphilis or gonorrhea, with the results, according to prison records, considered "gratifying."

By the mid-1930s the reformatory movement nationwide had waned. A world war and the depression had ousted the Progressive movement, and prostitution was no longer a major issue. Second and third generations of superintendents for the reformatories lacked the zeal of their founders, whose model prisons for women began to resemble custodial types of earlier decades. From that point on, more and more states abandoned the reformatory ideals and began building women's prisons based on the congregate models that housed males.

Niantic was among the exceptions. Under the charge of Elizabeth Munger, the Farm had become nearly self-sufficient. By the late 1930s, inmates were growing and harvesting their own food and selling a large surplus. In addition, four modern brick cottages were added, allowing the prison to expand its population and accept a wide range of women.

An article from a 1937 issue of the *Connecticut State Journal* summarized the prison's progress. "Combine a prison, a maternity hospital, a nursery, a hospital for the treatment of infectious diseases, a home for the unruly feeble-minded, a sanatorium for invalids, a mental hygiene clinic, and a place of cure for inebriates and drug addicts—combine them all into one, limit the inmate and staff in charge to the female sex, and there you have the Connecticut State Farm for Women, all in a single state institution." That year, inmates gave birth to forty-seven infants at the institution and fifty-six more infants were admitted with their mothers. By then, the maternity building contained six nursery wards with infants varying from a week to a year old. The journal article claimed that "the newborns are given the best of care and will be ensured their chance in life regardless of the stigma of illegitimate birth." After giving a glowing overview of the prison's accomplishments, the author, apparently a prison official, concluded, "Given proper support we could free every community in the state of such undesirable members."

By the 1940s, the population had climbed to 150, making it too costly for the prison to sustain itself as a working farm. Janet York, who began working at the prison as a college student in 1940, and later as a parole officer in 1949, recalled in a 1992 interview how the prison slowly started to disband the farm by cutting back on all the livestock, except for the cattle and chickens, but still maintained the gardens.

By 1948, the institution had more than a hundred infants in its care, and according to York, "an awful lot of the mothers weren't capable of taking care of the babies." The expense and responsibility of caring for the growing numbers of newborns prompted the state to phase out the nursery over the next two decades. From then on, inmates delivered their babies at area hospitals, and the children were placed in foster care or with relatives.

York became warden in 1960 and brought the Farm into a new era. During her tenure, the prison gradually phased out farm-related work and established its first high school equivalency program and college-level courses. Alcoholics Anonymous and Narcotics Anonymous groups, along with an alcohol- and drug-treatment program coordinated by Yale University, were also introduced.

In 1968, the Farm was placed under the jurisdiction of the state's newly created Department of Correction. After that, state farm matrons, as they had been referred to since the beginning, were called correction officers and given uniforms. In the next several years, affirmative-action policies brought in more minorities and male staff members.

Also during that time the state's civil liberties union named Warden York in a suit charging the Department of Correction with discrimination for holding women found guilty of "manifest danger of falling into vice," "lascivious carriage," and other archaic crimes. The laws were eventually declared unconstitutional and some fifty women were discharged from the Farm. Today York is in her seventies. A snappy, quick-humored woman, she recalls that everyone was relieved the issue had finally been resolved, adding, "the entire lawsuit was long overdue."

Throughout the 1970s, the prison served as a research incubator for many of the current psychological trends. The Harvard psychologist Lawrence Kohlberg set up a laboratory in one of the cottages to test his theory of moral development, which was covered by *Newsweek* magazine. Researchers from Yale and elsewhere employed behavior modification and other therapies in hopes of rehabilitating inmates.

By the time she resigned as warden in 1976, York had worked at the Farm for more than thirty years. She had come in at a time when the prison's self-sufficiency as a farm was in decline. Throughout its second era, she introduced more contemporary programs aimed at helping women survive on the outside, and teaching them how to become responsible for their actions. Overcrowding was not a problem and each inmate received plenty of emotional support. Though staff grappled with ways to cut down recidivism, according to York, "It was nowhere near the problem it is now." Assaults were nearly nonexistent and escapes, if they did occur, usually happened because an inmate felt she was needed back home to resolve a family crisis. It was a phase filled with fervor and optimism. "In the days when I was there it was a very relaxed atmosphere," York told me. "You really felt you were helping people. We had a lot of time to spend with these women. Now, no one has the time."

Surprisingly, the prison population dropped from 150 in the late-1960s to 125 in the mid-1970s. Though drug abuse was on the rise, mostly because of the heroin trade, the increase was not accompanied by violence. Few could predict that the advent of crack cocaine and stricter enforcement of drug laws would more than triple Niantic's population over the next fifteen years.

By the time Carol Dunn became warden in 1992, the overall prison population had swelled to more than six hundred, packing the cottages and forcing her to compensate for the overfill in York dormitory by placing extra mattresses on the floor of the cafeteria. By law, Dunn and every other warden in Connecticut were obligated to keep the inmate population below 110 percent of the prison's capacity—in Niantic's case, 618. If the maximum was exceeded for thirty days in a row, state law required the release of 10 percent of the convicts, those nearest the completion of their sentences.

As the only women's prison in the state at a time when the prison population was climbing at an unprecedented rate, the Farm had to engage in complicated maneuvering to keep a tight lid on the numbers. A new three-hundred-bed facility in Somers was intended as a second women's prison, but although construction had been completed, the state had no money to open it. In addition, the state had yet to approve funding to house women at one of the three minimum security prisons that had by law been made coed. Apart from a handful of transition programs and halfway houses, few alternative sanctions for women existed.

Given the slim options, in the summer of 1992, Dunn orders that a busload of inmates bound for court appearances be detoured to the Hartford Correctional Center for men, and housed overnight in a cellblock formerly leased to the federal government. The transfers begin after the inmate population has exceeded 618 for more than twenty days. In Hartford, the women are deloused and sleep on mattresses on the floor, while their beds in Niantic remain empty. The transfer allows Dunn to cut the inmate population to 618 and remain at legal capacity. Despite the criticism she receives from inmates, who view the action as inhumane, Dunn tells a reporter from the *Hartford Courant* that the wholesale release of more than 160 convicts with no supervision or treatment is a poor alternative, adding, "I don't think the public would be too happy with that."

In the same article, which appears on the top front page, JoNel Newman, a lawyer from the Connecticut Civil Liberties Union, which has long litigated for improved conditions at Niantic, calls Dunn's strategy "absolutely crazy," and "like putting a band-aid on an arterial wound." One of those transferred is featured in a photograph leaning against a pair of crutches. She describes having a broken hip and how her leg has been made worse from sleeping on a mattress on the floor, and how she is unable to get the pain killers given to her at Niantic to help her sleep.

In September, the strategy of transferring female convicts to the men's facilities is documented in a memorandum filed in federal court by the CCLU. The memo is added to the file of a longstanding lawsuit by women inmates against the state, a suit that resulted in a consent decree in 1988, governing housing conditions, population, and health services. Newman says she hopes the memo prompts the federal monitoring panel that oversees conditions at Niantic to act.

As the fall approaches, the overcrowding problems mount, and in parts of the prison, conditions verge on a state of emergency. In another desperate move to control the population, Warden Dunn turns the prison gymnasium in the old school house into a makeshift dormitory. Mattresses carpet the floor and portable bathrooms are brought in and placed on the stage. The place looks like a huge slumber party without the revelry. As the weeks pass, more inmates pour in, eventually swelling the gym's population above one hundred. The overnight transfers of inmates continue. By October, the number of women being transferred has risen to more than forty. Dunn continues to defend her actions by saying that few inmates have complained about the overnight transfers. In response to the negative press she is receiving, Dunn tells me, "I have nothing to hide. I'm not going to paint a wonderful picture of this place. I just hope people can distinguish between what's reality and what's bullshit."

The issue of overcrowding is only one of several challenges Dunn will face during her first year. For the first time in Niantic's history, gang affiliation is flourishing and Dunn estimates that there are at least twenty such groups. Though most are small-time neighborhood crews, others like The Nation, an African American band, and the Latin Kings boast members statewide. Because of the relatively small numbers of women "gangsters" nationwide, estimated to be about 10 percent, few studies are available that prison officials might use as guideposts to monitor gang maneuverings among females. Anne Campbell, who teaches at the Rutgers University School of Criminal Justice, has reported that female gangs seem confined to a bygone era in which women are perceived as the sexual slaves and criminal underlings of the males with whom they socialize.

Given the number of female gang members in Niantic who say they were raped or beaten by male gangsters, or that the men used them to sell or transport drugs, Dunn and others echo Campbell's observations.

Nevertheless, little attention has been given to female gangs once they land in prison. With few models available, correction officers and counselors can only speculate from experience how a female gang member might behave. Some feel that because most women in Niantic are mothers, and have more to lose than male inmates, that their gang connections, if any at all, will wane once they get to prison. Too, many of the women join gangs because of a boyfriend or family member and once that relationship is temporarily severed, they might lose interest in whatever is happening on the streets.

But others like Ellen Uhlein, a counselor for some 130 inmates in the Thompson Hall cottage, which houses unsentenced women and those sent to the Segregation Unit, disagree. "If you look at the big picture, you're dealing with people who are extremely manipulative, intellectually and emotionally," she tells me one afternoon. "And the higher the population, the more pressure there is for everybody." Given those variables and the evolution of prison gangs, she adds, "women are just as capable of that kind of [gang] bonding as men are."

Regardless of what anyone thinks, Dunn takes a cautious stance.

Though any gang affiliation poses a threat to the prison's stability, the Latin Queens far outnumber the others. Considered by federal and state law enforcement agents as the most ruthless gang in the state, the Latin Kings (female members are referred to as Queens) reportedly finance their organization through car thefts, weapons distribution, and drug trafficking. However, the King's charter prohibits members from using drugs. If caught doing so, they face suspension from the organization. Most recruits are in their teens and early twenties, with few job options and little education. Typical of many gang cultures, if a member is sent to prison, she is entitled to receive money, food, hygiene products, and emotional support. The organization, according to its members, gives them structure and some semblance of family. Indeed, members of the Latin Kings and Queens resent being labeled a gang and refer to themselves as "the Family."

Of the dozens of suspected Latin Queens in Niantic, the one considered the most dangerous, Margarita Biblioni, is in protective custody after receiving death threats from members of the organization who accused her of snitching. She has become famous throughout the prison as the Latin Queen Bee. A twenty-five-page affidavit, based on the testimony of one Latin King arrested in connection with a shoot-out at a Meriden housing project, named Biblioni as the regional commander for Waterbury. She denies it. State investigators have interrogated Biblioni twice in Niantic and tell Dunn she probably doesn't pose a threat to the prison, but that her stories contain some contradictions and she should be watched closely.

So far, correction officers have given Dunn only positive reports on Biblioni. She is highly cooperative and a hard worker, and she doesn't appear to be entangled in gang machinations. When Dunn and other officials question inmates about the Latin Kings and Queens, many fear talking about the organization. Others get defensive and say that "the Family's" main goals are getting kids off drugs and helping the Hispanic community. Some inmates report that Latin Kings have ordered Queens in Niantic to settle vendettas by beating or stabbing inmates who wrong them. Overall, police paint a picture of the Kings as an outlaw gang that murders, rapes, or maims members who try to leave the organization, and that recruits children as young as eight into the drug trade.

Sitting at her desk in the summer of 1992, only a few months into her new job, Dunn says she has nothing but disgust for the Latin Kings, and laughs sardonically when I ask her about the gang's purported philanthropic intentions. "These are people who treat women like property," she says. "And when the women in here say the Kings are a good organization I say, 'If that's true how many hospitals or day care centers have they built? How many scholarships have they awarded? What have they done to help the poor Hispanic?'"

After a pause, I tell her I plan to interview Biblioni in the Segregation Unit. "Just be careful," she says with a flash of irritation. "There are no better manipulators than these women."

5

The Stud and the Latin Queen

Laura Lago juggles a telephone receiver between her neck and chin while she writes up the last burst of activity inside the Segregation Unit, the Farm's prison within a prison. She jots down every transaction, from handing out sanitary napkins and towels to scheduling inmates' medical appointments. Having to record every movement that occurs on a post is as one of the more tedious tasks of a correction officer's life, but Lago handles it with finesse.

"This is a horror show today, honey," she quips to her colleague on the other line. "Everybody's goin' bonkers."

In the near distance, inmates pound on their cell doors while others swarm around her demanding medication and emotional support. At the end of her three-month rotation inside the prison's most clamorous and stressful unit, Lago's natural resilience has worn thin, and the strain shows. She suffers from dizziness and sharp, shooting pains in her arms. A lot of the time, she feels irritable and moody. Like every other guard who started working in Niantic before the 1980s, Lago has seen the Farm go from a bucolic reformatory to an overburdened holding tank mostly for drug addicts. The days of sitting down and letting an inmate unburden herself is a thing of the past.

Lago's inmates include one woman who has been coming to the prison since the early 1980s. Plagued with psychiatric problems partially tied to drug addiction, she swings from catatonic bliss to unexpected spurts of violence. As a teenager, the young woman volleyed

55

in and out of the state reformatory, where she once tried to commit suicide by setting herself on fire. She still carries the burn scars over most of her body. "She'd slit your throat and think nothing of it," Lago says. It is a clammy summer morning and we are sitting in the COs' office on the first floor with a couple of fans whipping the humidity around at high speed.

Lago tells me that the prison's most lethal inmate, Gabe Harris, spends most of her time in segregation for assaulting correction officers or inmates. A notorious repeat offender, her most recent round stemmed from an assault on her girlfriend, whom she tried to slice in half with a machete.

One anomaly among the current residents is Margarita Biblioni. The former social worker and mother of four is the only inmate placed in segregation under protective custody. She has never been to prison before. Her litany of charges includes possession of narcotics, possession of an illegal firearm, transporting a fugitive, and hindering prosecution.

To add to the chaos in the Segregation Unit, Lago and her partner Beth Racie have received a group of anti-abortion protesters who insist on being rolled down to segregation in wheelchairs as an act of civil disobedience. Correction officers liken the inmates to spoiled children, not because of their politics, but because of the inconvenience they cause an already overburdened staff. Once inside segregation they want special treatment, including a room with a toilet and sink. To keep them from disturbing the other inmates with their gospel songs and scripture readings, they get their wish.

The length of an inmate's stay in segregation depends upon the availability of a room, the discretion of the unit's lieutenant, and the seriousness of her wrong doing. Assault, possession of contraband, and sexual misconduct earn a fifteen-day or longer confinement; gambling or disruptive behavior carry a penalty of five to ten days. For twenty-three hours a day inmates remain locked in their rooms. They get fifteen minutes in the morning to shower, and forty-five minutes each afternoon to watch television. They wear green cotton smocks instead of civilian clothes. Smoking is prohibited. Despite the wall murals painted by former inmates, the unit looks like a turn-of-the-century hospital, poorly lit and smoke-stained, with worn-down tile floors. The nine rooms downstairs and eight upstairs each contain a chest of drawers and bunk beds. A few have toilets.

Inmates communicate with the outside prison population through couriers, women with green cards who wander the grounds freely, calling out and retrieving messages through the windows.

"Tell Julie I love her," one woman yelled down from segregation to a stocky friend earlier that morning, adding, "Tell that bitch Tracy when I get out of here I'm going to fuck her up."

Inside, inmates manage to pass "kites" or handwritten notes to each other, by asking COs to get them a towel or an aspirin, then slipping the note under the friend's door. Sex can also be arranged if two women are in the bathroom at the same time. Though it is risky and can result in further disciplines, inmates say that once they are inside the bathroom, COs often become so preoccupied with other matters that intimacy becomes easy. It is one of the perks of overcrowding, I'm told.

Lago and Beth Racie, who oversees the upstairs wing, operate out of offices at the end of each floor, both painted in pastels with rainbows above the windows. The intensity and pace of the place have gutted them both, and they are eager to receive their next assignment. Their tenure in segregation took a tragic twist early on when an inmate strapped a cord around a metal ceiling beam in her cell and hanged herself. In and out of the Farm for years, the young woman had been a drug addict with severe psychiatric problems and was rumored to have HIV.

When the suicide occurred, Lago was on her day off and in the process of moving into a new home. A colleague drove to her house and broke the news. It was weeks before she could walk into the cell where the young woman had died. "The day before her death I got a call from the medical unit saying Patty's coming back in," she recalls. "She was crying and upset and pacing around like a caged animal. She threw her arms around me and said 'Please Lago please, make my life stop hurting.'"

Perhaps, Lago adds, if COs assigned to segregation were allowed to give a cigarette to inmates under severe distress, instead of forcing them to wallow over their children and what a mess they've made out of their lives, such tragedies might be avoided.

"In the old days I'd give a woman a cigarette if I thought it would calm her nerves," Lago says. "But now if you give them food, candy, or cigarettes you could be fired."

The volatile nature of segregation makes the possibility of exposure to infectious diseases all the more real. At all times, correction officers carry rubber gloves and a mouthpiece that allows them to give mouth-to-mouth resuscitation without breathing in any saliva. Even then, it is easy to be caught off guard. COs tell of inmates spitting at them or tossing urine or feces in their faces when they open a cell door. An aggressive inmate will bite or scratch.

With her surehandedness, Lago has few problems dealing with some of Segregation's toughest inmates, like Harris, a twenty-five-year-old Jamaican woman with a record for assaults. Referring to herself as the Farm's "most dangerous stud," she struts through the halls with a cool-headed intensity, her muscular arms slightly bent at the elbows. On my way to see Biblioni, I run into her as she comes out of the bathroom. "You wanna hear my story?" she asks. Her offer seems too good to pass up.

A few minutes later, Lago opens the unit's television room, lets us in, then leaves, closing the door. Harris and I sit face-to-face, across a table. She places a brown paper bag on the table. Several seconds pass before she leans back in a metal chair and rocks slowly, methodically. Her eyes dart like starlings across the room, then stop and fix hypnotically on the floor before she speaks.

She tells me she grew up in Jamaica on a farm, where she once worked in her uncle's marijuana patch. Later, at age ten, she came by boat to the United States and found her way to Hartford. Her parents had both died by the time she was nine.

As a farm hand she perfected the use of a machete to cut stalks of marijuana. In Hartford she used it for protection and revenge. While in prison, she lashes out unpredictably at COs and inmates and spends most of her time in segregation as a result. It suits her well. The fewer inmates she has to confront the better.

Harris blames her behavior on a neurological disorder that requires daily doses of tranquilizers. "Without them I get cold sweats and the shakes and try to strike out at anybody," she says to me with icy assurance. "And you never want to see my bad side."

At home in Hartford, she worked on a garbage truck crew for the city's sanitation department. She lived in a house in East Hartford with her sixty-two-year-old husband and their two children, a five-year-old son and a four-year-old daughter. Harris's girlfriend of six years also lived with the family. In a way, she says, she likes coming to prison because it gives her a break from all of her emotional entanglements. She adds, "We had this routine. I'd spend three nights with my girl, three nights with my husband and one night alone. I hated the stress of it all."

When she first arrived in Hartford as a child, she alternated living with friends and relatives. At fourteen she was gang-raped and at fifteen she slept with her first woman. About the same time, her brother began serving a ten-year sentence in the state's maximum-security prison in Somers on a bank-robbery conviction. According to Harris, violence was a way of life in her community. "We come over here with nothing so we'll do anything to get what we want," she says. She defends the rise of the Jamaican Posses in Hartford, who have been tied to a recent series of bizarre revenge murders involving drugs.

"We love our guns," Harris says, adding that on the street she carried a .357 magnum and sometimes a .22-caliber handgun. "But my favorites are 9-millimeters, Smith & Wessons." Harris explains that the aggression stems not so much from choice as from lack of it. "It all comes down to poverty," she says, staring out a barred window that faces Bride Lake. "That's the reason for the violence."

In Niantic, she claims to have fashioned a reputation as a ladies' woman. But once a lover gets too serious with her or places any demands on her by asking a lot of questions, "I vanish," she says. Echoing what I have already heard from Katie Molina, she explains that in the lesbian culture there is a loosely defined hierarchy, typically headed by a black woman who thinks of herself as a stud. To become one usually requires returning to the prison several times to establish yourself. "If you're a stud, you can have as many women as you want," Harris says. "They usually have a wife, a mistress, and then a girl who just wants to be on the inside, who'll give you commissary and run errands for you."

Harris was let off from work early one Friday in the summer of 1990, then went to a mall to buy her girlfriend some earrings. When she arrived home, the stereo was blasting in the living room and her two children were asleep in a nearby bedroom. When she checked the back bedroom, she found her girlfriend in bed with a man who Harris refers to as her best friend.

"I ran to the closet and got a machete, then ran back into the bedroom," she says in a dispassionate tone. "I started swinging and tried to cut my girl in half, but only gave her a deep wound. I cut the dude in the leg. Then I called the ambulance, then I sat down next to my girl and she put her head in my lap and started to cry." She pauses, then smirks. "When my husband came home he couldn't figure out why there was blood all over the place."

The girlfriend, who survived the machete wound, makes regular visits to see Harris. Even so, Harris recently married a woman named Li Li, whom she met in segregation. The ceremony took place in the television room with another inmate serving as minister. "Li Li took my last name," she says proudly. She picks up the brown bag and pours dozens of love kites from Li Li across the table. "There was just something about her that made me want her," she says. "I just had to make her mine."

I ask Harris about a gang rape I heard she was involved in, in which someone purportedly shoved her fist up an inmate's vagina. She rolls her eyes and shakes her head. Finally she gives me a cool grin. "Look, we were all playing strip poker and that girl lost. We all knew what was goin' down."

Later that afternoon, Beth Racie sits at her desk on the second floor and logs in the number of Tylenols she has handed out to inmates. There appears to be a sweep of head, neck, and joint pains caused by the heat wave outside. In her early thirties, Racie possesses a mild and unassuming manner that inmates like, but the demands of overcrowding have spawned in her a deep cynicism.

"What happens is that you begin to distrust people," she says, picking at a salad she's ordered in from a local deli. "You get disgusted because you're dealing with drug addicts and prostitutes all day who don't take care of themselves. They come in here and get new glasses that the state pays for and dentures to replace the teeth they lost doing drugs. Every building you go to you see the same people over and over. We know they do drugs while they're here but we don't have enough staff to oversee it. For some of these women it's one big party."

Outside Racie's office, Margarita Biblioni has finished washing the hall walls and doorways, and returns a bottle of disinfectant to a closet. "Got anything else for me to do, Racie?" Biblioni says as she enters the office. Her consuming brown eyes harbor a fatigued sadness. Black roots sprout from her peroxided hair. There is a maternal dominance in her voice and gestures. She carries an inhaler to quell her asthma and uses it every few minutes to combat the stale air even the fans cannot stir. As a smoker in a smoke-free unit, she says she could sure use a cigarette.

A few moments later we sit alone in the television room. As Biblioni nibbles on a lunch of beans, rice, and a cheese enchilada, she recalls one morning the preceding April. At around 5:00 A.M., a band of federal and state agents charged through her apartment door with a battering ram, guns drawn. They searched the place for Latin King paraphernalia and found a .38 caliber handgun and a kilo of cocaine. The agents had been trailing her for months.

"If I went to the grocery store, they were behind me," she says. "They said I was the 'Ma' and was housing Latin Kings. Well, even if they were Kings, it didn't matter because I was everybody's Ma."

I knew several "Ma's" in the neighborhoods I had covered as a reporter. Biblioni fit the profile. Someone who was strident yet self-sacrificing, who went to extremes to protect her family, her friends, and their turf. In these neighborhoods unemployment ran 50 percent or more and most of the single-parent families were headed by women. They told me stories about police beating kids on their block and about cops on the take, who demanded a cut of the neighborhood's drug profits. The culture perpetuated its own brand of lawlessness.

Biblioni furrows her brow, leans in, and pounds her index finger on the table to make her point. Her eyes are red and swollen from crying. "They said I was the regional commander and the terminator for the state of Connecticut. They escorted me to Niantic with four state police cars in front, four in back. I rode in a big blue bus, like a sandwich. They closed every exit from Hartford to Niantic. The judge posted a $50,000 bond and I'm facing seven years in prison. I feel like I'm in a bad dream."

Her inmate classification and lack of disciplinary charges give Biblioni more freedom to move about. She spends most of her time writing letters, reading gossip magazines, and scrubbing the hallways and bathrooms. As a long-term resident in a short-term unit, her room has the only semblance of personality. She has placed trinkets, photographs of her children, and toiletries on her chest of drawers. The room smells of hand lotion.

Inmates come to her with their problems, and both Racie and

Lago comment about Biblioni's cooperative nature, a rare quality in segregation. Yet she knows her presence at the Farm makes Warden Dunn and other administrators nervous.

"When I first got here, they put me in segregation for sixteen days with no contact with my family. They thought I'd start recruiting and considered me a special risk. I guess they think I'm Al Capone or something."

Before moving to Waterbury in 1988, Biblioni had worked as a social worker for a Spanish community agency in Pennsylvania. Raised in Miami, she had come north with her children to pursue a better life. Then her sister asked her to move to Waterbury. "I figured that life was good here," she says. "But it obviously wasn't the dream that my sister had painted."

Like most cities in the Northeast during the late 1980s and early '90s, Waterbury's quality of life was in steep decline. Once a major brass manufacturing center, the city was now blighted by boarded-up shopfronts and factories, high unemployment within its urban neighborhoods, and crime. Each of the state's major cities suffered the same ills. Nevertheless, Connecticut stood out as a study in contrasts. While U.S. statistical data ranked the state as having the highest personal income per capita (due mostly to affluent Fairfield County), its largest cities—Bridgeport, Hartford, New Haven, and Waterbury—were consistently rated among the nation's poorest.

Given the climate, gangs like the Latin Kings, Los Solidos, and the Nation began to flourish in the inner cities. Block after block, gang insignias and painted eulogies of youngsters killed by gun violence stained the sidewalks and empty buildings. Members wearing colored beads or tattoos for identification stationed themselves on street corners and held secret meetings. Though the gangs attracted mainly young people, older family members often were drawn into the fervor, sometimes welcoming the financial contributions their children brought in from the streets.

Though street gangs were nothing new to American urban culture, having originated among Irish immigrants in the nineteenth century, never had there been so many, and never had their members been so young. Once limited to America's ghettos and barrios, gangs across the nation had expanded beyond their boundaries and emerged as a prominent subculture with their own languages and behavior codes. Experts including Carl Rogers, the vice president of the American National Council on Child Abuse and Family Violence, have pointed to the advent of crack cocaine in the mid-'80s as the most transforming element of street gangs. The drug's profit potential extended territories, increased violence, and turned gangs into drug-trafficking, criminal organizations.

The gangs in Connecticut exhibited a kind of schizophrenia. On the one hand, they extolled the virtues of education, discipline, and staying clean, while continuing to recruit children to sell drugs. I saw a number of children in the Hill section of New Haven go from being "spotters," careening up and down the streets on bicycles for around $100 a day on the lookout for cops and undercover agents, to being "runners," hiding and securing a gang's drug stash for some $500 a day, and eventually becoming street dealers, making up to $1,500 a day or more. With many of their families in shambles, their loyalties to the gang ran deep. Like stalwart missionaries willing to kill or die for the common cause, they found security and purpose within neighborhood posses (usually a group of kids who had grown up together), or city and statewide gangs like the Latin Kings.

Given its violent history, the "Family," as the Kings preferred to be called, warranted particular concern. Founded in Chicago in the 1940s as a fraternal organization, the Kings surfaced in Connecticut in the late 1980s when two inmates at the state's maximum-security prison at Somers, Nelson Millet and Pedro Millan, were granted permission by the Chicago Kings to start a Connecticut chapter. The men then composed what became known as the bible for the organization, a rambling, ungrammatical text with by-laws and rules prohibiting members from using drugs, committing thefts, assaulting other members, or discussing the organization with nonmembers.

According to Biblioni, she never intended to become entangled with the Latin Kings. Those that she knew of seemed to be crusaders for the community, helping to keep kids from hanging out on street corners and steering them away from selling or using drugs. But in the spring of 1991, things began to change. The Kings had established a chapter in Waterbury, where she lived in a poor neighborhood in the city's east end. During the day she worked as a receptionist for a credit collection agency. One evening, after she had gotten home from work, a young crew of Latin Kings stormed into her home with guns looking for her fifteen-year-old son. The boy had apparently gotten into a fight with one of them. They threatened to beat him when they saw him. Biblioni panicked. "My son didn't come home until later," she says. "The next day I drove him to upstate New York to my brother's where he stayed for a year until things cooled down."

Next, her brother-in-law, a Latin King, asked Biblioni to help resettle a woman named Elaine and her three children. She was told that the woman's husband was in jail and that the family needed help. Biblioni moved them into the apartment below her, painted it, and bought the family curtains and furniture. The two women became fast friends. But soon after they moved in, she noticed a flow of people going in and out of the downstairs wearing black and gold Latin King beads. When she questioned Elaine about it she learned that the woman's common-law husband was Pedro Millan, the co-founder of the Latin Kings. Considering Biblioni's street savvy, it is hard for me to imagine how she could have remained so oblivious to the gang's presence. Nevertheless, she insists she was clueless. Over the months, her contact with Millan's wife pulled her deeper into the Kings' hierarchy. Biblioni says she often spoke with Millan by phone when he was imprisoned in upstate New York for assault. Even then, she says, their conversations revolved around family matters, not business.

"At first I got very attached to Pedro," Biblioni recalls. "He was a very intelligent and warm person who hoped to return to put the Hispanic people to work. The Latin Kings painted a picture of him as the Godfather."

Biblioni's troubles began in April 1992 when a convoy of armed Latin Kings drove to a housing project in Meriden, Connecticut, to settle a dispute with a renegade faction. The confrontation resulted in a shoot-out, which left three men injured. According to police records, Millan ordered the shoot-out from prison and Biblioni was involved in the planning. In the next several weeks, a police sweep of the "Coronas" of the Waterbury chapter included Biblioni. After the raid on her apartment she was charged with illegal possession of drugs and a handgun. Biblioni claimed that the drugs were not hers, and that she had bought the gun on the street for protection.

After her arrest in April, a wave of paranoia swept through the Latin Kings as members accused each other of snitching to police. Members from the so-called negative faction of the organization issued orders to women in Niantic to have Biblioni killed.

"The Latin Kings I knew were all trying to do community service," she says. "Now somebody wants to kill Millan and they want to kill me. It all reminds me of the film *The Godfather*. Instead of seeing me as a mother, a sister, and a friend, I'm a gangster. They've convicted me before I've even gone to court."

When she first arrived at the women's prison, correction officers kept a cool distance. Thrown into the unit with the most vicious inmates and an oppressive atmosphere, she learned quickly about the hardcore realities of prison life. One morning after she arrived, an inmate jumped her from behind while she took a shower. "Right away, everybody thought I would retaliate," Biblioni says.

Her notoriety, deserved or not, spread throughout the general population. Some inmates in segregation began to resent her freedom from the restrictions they lived under. They called her names like Queen Bee and Miss PC (for protective custody). Other inmates revered her and sought her protection. One woman sent to segregation for assault walked up to Biblioni, kissed her hand, and asked for her blessing.

"Everybody's branded me like a cow," she says, pushing away the tray of cold enchiladas. "The police want to know who paid my rent and car payments. They said I was giving drugs to kids to sell. But the truth is, I had to sell all my jewelry to get $1,000 to pay a lawyer. My sister gave me $200 and Elaine gave me $300. Because of all this I lost my job and my home. I've never seen a psychiatrist before but I am now. This thing has destroyed me."

6

Biblioni's Goodbye

A couple of weeks after I talk with Biblioni, I stop by the Trumbulls, also known as the rumbling Trumbulls, because of the units history of inmate fights. I've been told by COs and inmates that the unit houses several Latin Queens, one of whom is the "sister-in-law" of Nelson Millet, the cofounder and the "supreme crown president" of the Kings. In the corner of the cafeteria, Alicia Gutierrez from Bridgeport sits with three other Queens smoking cigarettes. At first, Alicia glares at me suspiciously, but when I tell her I have had a conversation with Biblioni, she lets down her guard. She has large brown eyes with dark circles underneath; she's twenty-two going on forty. She is eager to talk about the Kings. From her posture and eye contact with the other Queens, it's clear she's in command. She takes charge of the conversation.

When she was thirteen, she tells me, Nelson Millet moved in with her mother and brought along his twenty-six-year-old brother. In the nine years since, she has had three children with him, and calls herself Nelson's sister-in-law. Now, she says, her common-law husband is at the Whalley Avenue jail in New Haven on assault charges. Nelson is in prison in California for armed robbery. Alicia has been in and out of Niantic for the past five years on larceny, assault, and violation of parole convictions. She has been sent to segregation for assault five times.

I want to know how much influence the Kings have over the Queens in Niantic. Alicia gives a half grin and tosses back her hair. "If we have problems we try to solve them ourselves before we take them to the Kings," she says. "They did order us to beat up one woman who was going with a King, because she slept with a woman in prison. And when they tell us to do something, we do it."

A thirty-nine-year-old Latin Queen sits next to Alicia. She has just started her bid for drug charges. After getting the nod from Alicia, she explains the Kings' hierarchy. "There's the president, vice president, regional commander, chief enforcer, and sergeant of arms, who's like the right hand to the president." She adds that the Queens in Niantic do not carry weapons. "We don't have to because we have use of the curling irons." They do not see any conflict between the Kings' ban on using drugs and their arrests for selling drugs.

Throughout our conversation one of the other Queens cries sporadically because she has just received word that her children are being put up for adoption. After a few minutes, her emotions overcome her and she leaves the room.

Alicia says she stays in the organization because it is her family and "because everybody knows me and makes me feel important." She invites me to attend one of their meetings the following Sunday afternoon.

When the time comes, I go to Alicia's room, but when I get there, she tells me they have to go upstairs to another Queen's room. Within the past several days, Alicia has received word that she has been suspended from the Latin Kings for getting high while on a furlough and therefore cannot lead the meeting. Alicia joins the four other Queens anyway. She is subdued and slides into a corner of the bunk bed, curls up, and wraps her arms around her knees.

The leader of the meeting, Lucy, who had left the cafeteria in tears, is much more composed. The women begin by saluting, raising their index and pinkie fingers in the air and calling out, "Amor." For a few minutes, they talk about their children and other Queens in Niantic who need help. The meeting seems rehearsed and awkward. They look at me every few seconds as if they are waiting for me to ask them a question. Finally I do.

Biblioni, I'm told, is the president of the Queens in Niantic. Through kites distributed from the Segregation Unit she issues orders and messages to her Latin Queens. She is not to be crossed.

In the foyer of the medical unit the air is heavy with the smells of antiseptic and old food. Little seems to have changed in the way of decor since the days when women were quarantined here and given injections of mercury or arsenic to cure their syphilis. Dingy yellow corridors, bleakly lit and cracked in spots, swallow up the inhabitants. A bedraggled woman in her thirties with large scabs on her face and legs lumbers down the hall toward her room. She is wearing a pink terry cloth robe, half-tied at the waist. As she passes, she stares at my note pad, then calls out over her shoulder, "You writin' a book on this place? You should call it 'The Prison from Hell.'" Her quip does not appear to phase the male CO sitting behind the reception desk. He barely looks up from the magazine he is reading.

Seconds later, Margarita Biblioni appears from a doorway at the end of the long corridor and smiles as she walks to greet me. She spreads her arms wide, then embraces me like an old friend. Her face is sallow and drawn and she has put on weight. The CO takes us to a room, empty but for a set of bunk beds and two chairs. He closes the door.

"It's my forty-third birthday," she says wiping her eyes. She sits on the bottom bunk facing me. "The last place I thought I'd be spending it is in here." I had not seen her for nearly three months. Every time I visited the Segregation Unit she was either in the medical unit because of her asthma, or in the hospital in New London. The hospital stay came after three court appearances in Waterbury where the judge never showed up. Each time she waited it out in a courthouse cell, handcuffed and shackled. "The press was always outside the courthouse waiting for me," she says. "This one female reporter was a real bitch. She'd been following me ever since my arrest. She called me the Queen Bee and asked me if the Latin Queens in Niantic were under my wing. I refused to talk to her."

The prolonged stress of the ordeal aggravated her asthma and caused her lung to collapse. The two weeks she spent in the hospital gave her time to reflect on her past and plan for her future. After her arrest, vandals ransacked her apartment and stole her furniture and a collection of porcelain figurines. It hit her hard that once she gets out of prison she will have to start from scratch. Now back in the claustrophobic atmosphere of the medical unit, the reality of her life comes crashing down on her like never before. "I have nothing," she says, pulling a tissue from inside the arm of her sweater. Her fingernails are chewed ragged.

Her children and sisters had come to visit her a few days before.

They spent most of the time in the Visitors' Center crying. A CO sat with them the whole time and monitored the conversation. "She wouldn't even let me touch my kids, which was hell," she says.

By late fall, the conspiracy and other charges against Biblioni in connection with the Meriden shoot-out have been dropped, leaving her with the charge of possession with intent to sell. She returned to the Segregation Unit and kept herself busy. Within a few weeks, she'd painted the entire first floor white, then decorated it with a red striped border. Next she stripped and waxed the floors. The entire project took her about 120 hours. It kept her mind off cigarettes.

During that time, a woman came into the unit suffering from a severe depression because she feared she would never see her children again. She sought out Biblioni, who consoled her and tried to lift her spirits. One day, while she was cleaning the hallway, Biblioni decided to look in on the woman. After knocking on her door and receiving no reply, she looked through the window at the top of the door and saw the woman hanging from a ceiling pipe. "Her face was bright red," Biblioni recalls during our final interview. "She had foam coming from her mouth, she looked like she was going to explode."

Biblioni screamed for help. Within seconds, she and the correction officers on duty disentangled the woman and rushed her to the medical unit where she was stabilized. For a week after the incident, Biblioni took tranquilizers and had nightmares about dying in prison. Warden Dunn later congratulated her and gave her 120 days of good time for saving the woman's life and for doing all the work in the Segregation Unit.

Another time Biblioni sat in her room during "lock" reading a *People* magazine about Woody Allen and Mia Farrow's child custody battle. Just as she began to doze off, she heard voices in the main office next to her room, and then some loud thuds. She thought it was an inmate going off on a CO. In a panic she pounded on her door to get out, but no one came. She got so frustrated that she punched her hand into the chest of drawers. By then, the COs overseeing segregation had become her friends and she wanted to protect them from attacks by inmates. On one hand, she'd seen the attempted assaults on COs and seen the verbal abuse they had to endure. On the other hand, she had heard a male CO yell obscenities to the women and treat them like dirt. Sometimes, she says, it's difficult to tell the difference between the criminal and the cop. Overall, she adds, the COs she has met are pretty decent people. She would come to their rescue if she were needed.

It turned out that the noises coming from the office, were not threatening, just the commotion from several people in one room. For days after, Biblioni stared at her swollen hand and thought maybe the insularity of segregation and the pressures of her case were causing her to go insane. Like so many of the other inmates in segregation, she figured she too was losing it.

On a cool autumn afternoon before Thanksgiving, Biblioni discusses her "nightmare disguised as a life." She is sitting in the television room cleaning silverware and folding napkins. Apart from the telephone ringing in the front office, the unit is calm. Her only visitor, the prison chaplain, has just left. He always comes in carrying a department store bag filled with colored plastic rosaries and scapulas. Because Biblioni is not allowed to go to Mass, he says prayers with her and lets her talk about her predicament.

"He comes here when he can," she says. "And he always leaves me with the impression that something is haunting him."

As she slides her fingers across the paper napkin creating a smooth, rectangular crease, she thinks about what she will do three weeks from now when she gets out. Her sister is setting her up in a condo outside Waterbury, away from everyone. Biblioni just wants to be isolated. She will be serving out the rest of her time through a supervised home-release program until the end of 1993, and hates the thought of having to hang around Waterbury. If she could, she would take her kids, "get the hell out of this area," and move down to Florida near her parents. Her mother is Spanish, and her father is Italian. The unrelenting winds from Hurricane Andrew the previous summer had pounded their neighborhood, leaving their home badly damaged. They kept a small aviary in their back yard, and when the storm hit it destroyed the cages and all the beautiful exotic birds flew away. Her father is crushed. Biblioni is in Niantic and cannot get through to them because the phone lines are jammed. At a time when her parents desperately need her support she is in jail, for reasons she cannot even begin to explain to them.

When I ask if she is the president of the Queens in Niantic, Biblioni laughs. Recently she has been watching the news and has seen a file clip of herself getting out of a police van, handcuffed and shackled, in a story about the crackdown on gang crime in Connecticut. "The media has created this myth of me like I was high up in this organization," she says. "It's the same way here." Women will intentionally act up in the cottages just to get tossed into segregation, so they can meet her. Inmates come to her and ask for her blessing. Make me a Queen, make me a Queen, they plead. At the same time, many of the black inmates hate her. "They think I'm in here because I'm a snitch," she says. "They think I'm getting special treatment. They'll walk by the windows and yell up 'Hey Miss PC, the Latin Queens ain't shit.'"

Biblioni is dressed in a gingham shift and a tattered beige cardigan sweater. She leans back and combs her fingers through her thick hair. "I get women shouting things up to my window constantly. They yell, 'Hey Marge, so and so says hi,' or 'this Queen says hi,' or somebody else. I don't even know these people."

Because of her connection to Millan she knows a lot about the Latin Kings; how sophisticated they are; how there are maybe eight thousand in the whole state. They have people from all walks of life including lawyers, doctors, businessmen, and computer experts. "These girls in here don't even know the meaning of this organization," she says.

Her main concern are two Latin King brothers from Waterbury named Jose and Luis. They have threatened her life. Jose was among the fifty Kings armed with guns, bats, and knives who stormed the Meriden housing project. In a sworn statement to police, Jose later named Biblioni as the regional commander of Waterbury, while other Kings told police she helped to orchestrate the shoot-out.

To explain why they hate her, Biblioni describes a showdown she had with Luis in a Waterbury park that spring, in which she criticized him for disgracing the organization by making violent threats to people and recruiting young boys to sell drugs. "We met in this secluded area and about fifty people came with me and stood by my side," she says. "Luis had only about ten people backing him up. I told him, 'I don't care who the fuck you think you are.' His reply was, 'This is a man's world and as a woman you have no right to make decisions.'"

When she walked away from Luis, the crowd of supporters followed her. "I didn't expect all this support from people. After it was over, I didn't know what to do with all of them."

She stresses again and again that the only reason she fell into the inner circle of the organization is because she helped out Pedro Millan's common-law wife and their children. Throughout her life, people have always seen her as a rock and leaned on her. Now she thinks maybe that's not such a healthy attribute.

"My sister is afraid Luis is going to hurt me when I get out of here," she says, "but I have protection and I'm not afraid. I've always been fearless."

When the state police interrogated her, they told her that Pedro Millan had married a man in prison. She says she doesn't know if they did that to manipulate her, or what, but it really doesn't matter. She is disillusioned with the Latin Kings and does not trust Millan anymore, anyway. The Kings lied to her, and turned against her. Nelson Millet, who represents the "good element" of the Kings, she says, has asked her to become a regional commander when she gets out. She has declined.

"After all this humiliation, I just want to keep a low profile and get out of this state as soon as I can," she says.

In the seven months she has been in prison, she has learned a lot about human nature, and one thing is for certain, nobody is going to take advantage of her again. "I just can't wait to go to my own refrigerator and grab a soda and sit on my own couch and smoke a cigarette," she says. "I'm tired of eating noodles and lettuce that looks like it's been stepped on. I'm tired of looking through bars. It's bad for the eyesight."

The week Biblioni goes home, Laura Lago and Beth Racie are working a rotation in Fenwick South. It is the first time they have worked together since leaving the Segregation Unit a few months before. Lago comments about the day-and-night difference between segregation and Fenwick South, where it is calm and the women are used to having things their way. As they sit in the front office checking out curling irons and cleaning supplies, they recall the bizarre experience of their three-month shift inside seg: the suicide of an inmate, the explosive behavior of Gabe Harris, the stress of anti-abortion protesters, and the legacy of Margarita Biblioni. The week Lago left the unit, she adds, she collapsed and was rushed to the hospital for blood pressure-related problems.

"I liked her," Lago says about Biblioni between phone calls and requests for cigarettes. "She just seemed like somebody who took care of everybody in the neighborhood and because of that she got railroaded."

Around the time of Biblioni's release, the prison chaplain, Biblioni's only visitor and sole spiritual support, is escorted by police off the prison grounds for reportedly having sex with a male inmate in a nearby prison. An article appears in *The Day*, the New London daily, a few days later, noting that he had been arrested for similar activities in Rocky Neck State Park.

Warden Dunn is on the phone when I visit her office soon after. "I'm so sorry things aren't going so well at home," she says in a comforting tone. When she gets off the phone, she mumbles that she was speaking with a staff member undergoing marital problems. Then she tells me how harried everything is because the prison's annual inspection is the next day. She will not talk about the priest and will only say about Biblioni, "Well, she prevented a suicide and didn't do anything here to promote gang activities, and that's what I was most concerned about."

7

Delia's Desire

As Delia's parole hearing date draws nearer, the whole unit, inmates, COs, and Keck, the counselor, keeps a watchful eye. In typical fashion, Delia diverts the conversation away from herself and draws out stories from others, trying to appear as if nothing is out of sync. Inmates tell her tales about the Latin Queens and she decides there is probably both good and bad among them. She knows not to get too excited. When Erica Huggins and other Black Panthers were thrown into Niantic during Delia's first bid in the early 1970's, they caused a lot of ruckus too, she recalls. A lot of it turned out to be theater, which is probably also true of the Latin Queens. Huggins and her comrades sat segregated for their entire sentence. Yet it was other inmates who were planting the seeds of hysteria, wanting to stage sit-ins and all that nonsense, as Delia put it.

She turns her attention to long chats with her friends or calms herself by reading the Bible, writing letters, and listening to gospel tapes. Other inmates who have gone before the Board of Parole help to ease her mind by telling her it isn't as bad as the grilling one gets from the Board of Pardons, which is like going through an actual trial. Still, the thought of sitting exposed in front of a panel of strangers who know the raw traumas of your life from reading through volumes of court documents, is not something Delia can dwell on for very long.

"I just hope I don't have to talk about Darryl and all that other stuff," she says one October morning as she fills a plastic bucket with a bar of soap, some lotion, and a rolled-up towel, and heads into the shower. "I just hope they'll be gentle."

Nevertheless, she prepares herself. In the weeks leading up to the November hearing, Delia organizes her file several times and tries to imagine the questions she might be asked. Several friends and relatives write letters in her support. Probably the most poignant and valuable contribution is a letter written by Peter Scilliari, the public defender from New London who had represented Delia after she stabbed her son to death in 1985. Detailed and emotional, the two-page, single-spaced statement began by mentioning the two dozen interviews Scilliari and his staff conducted in preparing Delia's defense.

In the opening paragraphs he summarized Darryl's character: "Our investigation disclosed that the decedent was universally regarded as an extremely assaultive individual who, for whatever reason, spent his life engaging in abusive, cruel, destructive and frequently felonious behavior."

Later, the letter described, through a litany of witnesses' testimony, how Delia had become the target of her son's aggression: "He seemed to delight in humiliating her in front of family and friends. He once beat her at a family picnic, leaving her face swollen and her body bruised. On another occasion she held a homecoming dinner party for him, which ended with him pouring scalding spaghetti sauce on her, pinning her to the floor, and mashing it in her face. He frequently beat and bruised her, spit in her face, stole or demanded money to buy drugs, and broke down her door when she tried to lock him out of her home." And while Delia had made attempts to get help for herself and her son by moving from New Haven to the relative quiet of New London, and had called the police the night of the incident, it seemed that nothing could curtail the inevitable. Scilliari continued, "With a single thrust, one nightmare ended and another one began."

Her sister Myrt and nephew Jerry also wrote letters, painting Darryl as a Jekyll-Hyde character who mistreated his mother to extremes. Delia cannot pick up the letters without crying. Unlike many inmates who are eager to reveal every detail of their shattered lives, she guards the topic of her tragedy and avoids talking about the beatings or other abuse. She mentions her son's name only in a harmless context. Once, while watching a news report about the owner of a New Haven funeral parlor who was under investigation for covering up his failure to bury the body of a local woman, Delia piped up, "They're the ones that embalmed Darryl." After a short pause she added half-jokingly, "God only knows where the poor boy is," then changed the subject.

Occasionally when she shows a visitor her stack of family photographs, she pulls out a picture of Darryl. It shows the young man sitting on a porch step, his long legs stretched out in front of him, his elbows resting on his knees. He is wearing a tank top and shorts and is aglow with that all-embracing smile, just like his mother's. Next to him sits Charlie Gorham, Delia's common-law husband. The mood in the picture suggests they could be kin or just good friends enjoying a sunny summer afternoon.

But according to court testimony, the image captured in the photograph masked a vicious reality. Delia and Gorham "were virtual hostages in their own home, and she felt helpless to protect herself from him [Darryl]," wrote attorney Scilliari. One evening while high on drugs, Darryl nearly beat to death the sixty-three-year-old Gorham with an ashtray stand. He spent several weeks in the hospital with broken bones in his face.

According to witnesses, Delia pressured her husband not to file a criminal complaint after the incident, and when other such incidents occurred, she often packed up and stayed with friends instead of having Darryl removed from her home. Seven years in prison did not change her loyalty and devotion to her son. Although the public defender and others painted her son as a monster, Delia protects his memory by saying little more than, "Darryl was always a good boy. There wasn't anything wrong with him. I mean it. It was the drugs that made him mean. The drugs turned him mean."

While most women in Niantic who had killed their batterers are earning sympathy from the news media and women's rights groups, Delia's case is complicated by her previous manslaughter conviction and a history of assault charges. No one can predict how that might affect the Board of Parole's decision.

Throughout the fall, she isolates herself inside Fenwick South. She stops going to church on Sundays because of the growing concern about gangs and the increased security at services. She also feels that a lot of women go to church to meet girlfriends or cop drugs. "Seeking any kind of spiritual guidance is the last thing on these people's minds," she says.

Instead of attending church, she often finds solace in the afternoons by sitting on the screened porch that abuts the living room, and watching the wildlife and the changing fall foliage. Inmates often stroll by, coming and going from the medical unit or on their way to or from school. But since it is difficult to decipher from the outside who is on the porch, Delia maintains her privacy. There is also an unspoken rule among Fenwick South residents that the porch is sanctuary where a person's privacy is not to be violated.

Given Delia's popularity among the women as a friend and consoler, a place to rest her mind is essential. Most of the day, someone stands outside her door waiting to talk with her. An inmate knows to knock only when her light is on, which it is most of the time. But when new residents of Fenwick South seek her out, Delia often greets them with suspicion. As with anyone she doesn't know, she is cordial and talkative, but at the same time, she scans the person's face and body for any clues of disingenuousness. "You've always got to be on the watch for snitches," she'd say. "They're all over the place." Delia shuns anyone who tells on other inmates or provides COs with inside information in exchange for favors. Even women she considers daughters she refuses to talk to if word gets back to her that they have snitched on someone. When one daughter, who had told officials that a male CO was having an affair with her roommate, greets Delia at church one Sunday, the sixty-year-old matriarch tells the young woman she cannot talk to her anymore because she has no respect for a snitch. Although Delia doesn't approve of the affair, disclosing it to officials, in her mind, is a much more serious matter.

Women often stroll by her window to say hello and give her an update on their lives and release status. Delia always shouts, "Hey, where've you been?" in a way that makes her visitor feel special and worried over. Occasionally, Delia's old acquaintance Bobbie Moore, whom she met in the late 1960's yells to her from the road outside Delia's window. Bobbie has been in and out of the Farm for a series of drug possession and trafficking charges. As a long-termer, such a pattern sticks in Delia's craw. "I can't stand how she goes in and out of here like it was some party while I just sit," she'd say whenever Bobbie's name came up. At the same time, she finds her old friend highly entertaining.

A gregarious personality with a flair for bending the truth, Bobbie tells tales of working for the mafia and of being the first person to sell packaged heroin in New Haven. She speaks of channeling drugs from South America and the Caribbean to Connecticut and of how she once robbed a jewelry store and was never caught. One day, while sitting in a counselor's office in the Trumbull South cottage and boasting about her criminal acumen, Bobbie paused, raised one hand in the air and covered her heart with the other, rolled her eyes, and muttered a soulful, "Lord, I'm here waitin' for ya." She then broke into a wicked laugh, stopped, breathed deeply, and stiffened into a trancelike quiet before saying, "One day a big white chariot's gonna come down and sweep me away from here."

She suffers from acute diabetes, and experiences periodic spells of blindness. "When my sugar gets too low," Bobbie said, "It knocks my lights out."

On Sundays, Bobbie dresses for church as if it were a royal banquet and she, the matron of honor. She strolls into the prison chapel with her head held high, wearing white silk pants and a matching jacket, a white hat with a five-inch brim, gold high heels, gold looped earrings, and gold-plated sunglasses. She sways to the gospel music, her hands raised high, her eyes closed. While the preacher's staccato message hammers on, sending some of the women into convulsions, Bobbie keeps a steady, delirious rhythm, calling out "Jesus, Lord!" every few minutes.

Delia's and Bobbie's history at the Farm, and the fact that both women are African American with roots in the deep South, created a bond between them that has lasted close to twenty years. Unlike in the early days, however, when there were fewer rules to separate them, the women now communicate mostly through other inmates. And nowadays, their communications consist mostly of Bobbie boasting to Delia about how well she has been doing on the outside. Once, when Bobbie returned to prison after violating parole for not showing up for her work-release program at a McDonald's in Hartford, she circulated word back to Delia that she had actually managed the restaurant. When the news reached Delia, she broke into a chuckle and said, "Manager? Who's she foolin'? That woman can't even read."

Every month or so, Delia takes a furlough either to New Haven, New London, or Boston where she has relatives. Her only living kin from her immediate family is her older sister, Myrt, who has cancer and lives in Boston. Delia has a brood of nieces and nephews and godchildren, some of whom write and visit her regularly. Many times when she goes on furlough, particularly during holidays, she ends up cooking for family gatherings of twenty or more people. At such events, liquor flows with abandon, and Delia will later describe how she keeps herself entertained by sitting down after dinner in a corner chair where she can watch people "getting goofy and making fools of themselves." As far as she is concerned, alcohol has ripped her life apart and she has spent the last eight years paying for her excesses. She once returned from a furlough with alcohol on her breath, prompting prison officials to suspend her furlough privileges, which she considered unjust. "All that was was mouthwash that I used to rinse with before I returned and they mistook it for alcohol," she insists.

Nowadays, however, as Delia counts the hours until her parole hearing, she wonders if she is not better off inside the Farm's cloistered confines. She keeps her television mumbling nearly all the time to block out the noise in the cavernous hallways and to ensure privacy in her conversations with visitors. But during the fall of 1992, she begins to pay particular attention to the carnage taking place in the New Haven neighborhoods where she has been raised. Nearly every day the noon and six o'clock broadcasts, report on the new culture of the inner city, a culture in which youngsters tote 9 mms and kill over drugs, girls, or sneakers. News coverage of grieving mothers reacting to the aftermath of drive-by shootings or babies shot dead by stray bullets becomes an everyday occurrence.

New Haven now has at least five major drug gangs, with names like the Jungle Boys, Kensington Street International, and the Island Brothers. The Latin Kings have placed a stranglehold on the Fair Haven section of the city. Through the cafeteria grapevine and COs, Delia continues to hear stories of inmates whose sons, husbands, or boyfriends have been murdered over drug deals gone sour. For those like Delia, who have been serving time since the mid-eighties, right when the crack cocaine trade began infiltrating the Northeast, the bizarre and senseless devastation that flashes across the television screens inside the cocoon of Fenwick South only increases anxieties about having to return one day to the outside.

In addition, Delia enjoys her status at the Farm. Everyone I talk to knows her or knows of her as a sort of living legend. Even the COs dote on her and call her Miss D. Some she calls her "special" COs, ones who will smuggle in submarine sandwiches and sweets to her and seek her advice if their personal lives need mending. One night while she is reading her Bible, Delia is visited by a young male CO, who is shaken because his father, suffering from brain cancer, has only a short time to live. "I grabbed his hand and he started to cry," she recalls. "He said I was the only person in Niantic who knew about it. The thing is, I know a lot of what goes on here and always have. But it's always been that way with me. Even when I was plastered all the time, people would tell me things."

Her old friend next door, Bonnie Foreshaw, provides Delia with hours of good conversation. Late into the night the women visit each other's rooms, eat candy, and exchange gossip and personal concerns. Raised in a housing project in Miami's Liberty City, Bonnie often talks about how the women in her family have endured generations of physical and mental abuse. She usually wears long dreadlocks, flecked with silver, tucked into a Kufi hat, or Muslim skull cap, as a sign of modesty. As a religious observance, she dresses in skirts, never trousers. Bonnie has a nobility about her that inmates admire. She too, has a covey of "daughters," mostly young women with leanings toward Mohammedanism. At forty-five, she stands close to six feet tall, and speaks in soft, articulate phrases, weaving in axioms from Eastern philosophies. Books shape her approach to life, in particular those of Alice Walker, Thomas Merton, Toni Morrison, Thich Nhat Hahn, J. Krishnamurti, and anything exploring the history of Rastafarianism.

Over the years that she has lived in Niantic, Bonnie has made several attempts to have her case reopened based on her charge that because her court-appointed lawyer was incompetent, she received an unfair trial. She has procured mostly legal-aid lawyers, who, for various reasons, never followed through on her habeas corpus appeal. Although admitting that she fired the bullet that killed a woman she did not know, she claims she did so to defend herself against a man who was threatening her. In early 1992, Mary Werblin, a lawyer from Litchfield County in the state's northwest corner, took up Bonnie's case. Convinced that Foreshaw had received an unfair trial, Werblin is reviewing hundreds of pages of court documents on a pro bono basis and hopes to get the cased reopened.

As an inmate, Bonnie takes up the cause of raising the women's awareness about abuse. She publishes an editorial in the local newspaper on the importance of battered women's shelters, and speaks movingly about her own life to radio talk-show hosts and local film-makers.

"I was a prisoner long before I was an inmate," she once said to me, during a discussion about the large numbers of women in Niantic with histories of abuse. She then added, "So many of us here are victims of circumstance. All it takes is a fraction of a moment and you could be sitting here and I could be you."

One late afternoon as we sit in her room, she tells me that her stepfather had sexually molested her at the age of eleven. She hoped that by telling her mother the man would be thrown out of the house. Instead she was sent from her home to live with an aunt. At twelve, she had her first child. From that point on, her life revolved around a series of violent relationships with men. "My relationships never started out as abusive," she says. She has the beginnings of a migraine headache and has hung a blanket over her window to shade out the fading light. "The behavior developed gradually and got worse and worse. It finally got me to the point where I was psychologically traumatized."

Five days a week she works in the commissary office, recording inventory in the computer. She also works as a reporter for the "Niantic Voice," the prison's newspaper. Once a month she meets with Warden Dunn as part of a committee on inmates' concerns. Much of her spare time she spends in the lounge of the cottage, sitting in front of the television with a bundle of needlework in her lap. Each year she makes dozens of colorful sweaters, blankets, and capes for her children and grandchildren.

Before coming to Niantic, she had owned her own home and had worked for ten years as a machinist at a wiring manufacturer in Hartford, where she also served as a shop steward. If she could live her life over again, she often says, she would have left Connecticut long ago and moved to the Caribbean and opened a guest house for tourists. Under the soothing sun, she would have lived a quiet, spiritual life. "Yet instead I sit here day after day dealing with all of these wounds inside my head. The kinds of wounds that never heal."

Delia knows that Bonnie faces a long battle but gives her as much support as she can. Of the two women, Delia is certainly the stronger and more realistic. While Bonnie has a moody nature and doesn't adjust well to changes in prison routine, Delia accepts as inevitable the unpredictability of prison life. Every so often, however, an inmate will come to her complaining about a new rule and ask her to persuade the COs to change it. "A lot of people are afraid of me because of my outspoken ways," Delia says to me one day. "If something's going wrong I'm not going to take that." Once, when a new CO tried to ban the women from having a loaf of bread in the television room as they had been allowed to do for years, Delia went straight to the woman and said, "Look, the women have had that loaf of bread in here forever and they're used to going in and making peanut butter and jelly sandwiches whenever they feel like it." She takes a deep breath. "And that's the way I am, I speak up about things."

While some COs like the quiet pace of Fenwick South, a few clash with inmates who live there, calling them the Fenwick Princesses, because as long-termers they are set in their ways and don't tolerate new rules and regulations easily. And why should they? Delia will ask. The women of Fenwick South work hard to ease the misery of confinement by making the unit their home and minding their own business. For some new CO to come in and ban a customary practice seems like vindictiveness more than anything else. "You better believe that being locked up and at the mercy of these people is hell," Delia says whenever anyone notes how well she coped as an inmate.

More than anything else, she wants her own home again, where she can cook and sleep without being disturbed. To make parole she knows she has to come up with a plan setting forth the specifics of her living arrangements. Although she knows it is sketchy, she plans to move in with her goddaughter who lives in New London with her nineteen-year-old son. Everything else she needs for parole, court papers, recommendations from friends, and evaluations from prison officials make it appear that she has made tremendous strides in reforming her behavior.

At 9:00 A.M. on November 12, 1992, Pasquale Mangini, the head of the state's parole board, accompanied by two other parole board members and a clerk, sets up the day's files on a long, oak table in a conference room in the administration building. With french doors and bookcases, the room has an air of formality about it. Every month the board meets here to review and decide the cases of inmates at the Farm and inmates from the male prison down the road. Until the board calls their names, inmates stay in a nearby waiting room, where interactions between the men and women are closely monitored.

A Jamaican woman in her mid-twenties is the first to go before the board. Serving two and a half years for possession of drugs, assault, and breach of the peace, she sits calmly with her legs crossed in a chair facing the board. Her name is Sandra and the board has decided before the hearing to deport her. "You have the right to contest this decision," says Mangini, a silver-haired man with soft eyes and a direct glare. The woman nods her head and says she wants to go back.

"What do you plan to do when you get back to Jamaica?" another board member asks.

"I haven't been there since I was thirteen, but I'll stay with relatives and work as a nurse's aide," she answers.

After Mangini tells the young woman that her parole will become effective December 1, the board members wish her luck and then take a short recess.

Meanwhile, Delia has been brought by a van to the administration building. Aided by Donna Henry, her counselor, and two prison advocates from the Connecticut Prison Association, Delia climbs a steep flight of stairs clutching a cane. She wears a red damask dress with a blue blazer, gold and pearl earrings, and a gold cross. One of her daughters in Sleepy Hollow has styled her hair so that it sweeps back in tiny waves. To relieve her swollen feet, caused by poor circulation, she wears loose-fitting pink bedroom slippers. Once she makes it to the second floor, Delia sits down on a chair in the hallway and takes a deep breath.

Tucked away in the sleeve of her blazer she carries a handkerchief, which she uses to mop her brow. Within minutes, the clerk calls her and her party into the room. She sits in the same chair as the inmate before her and rests both hands on top of her cane. As the board riffles through her files, Delia shifts nervously in her chair. The proud stature that she displays in Sleepy Hollow has all but vanished as she faces the three parole board members.

As part of the proceeding's protocol, Mangini reads off her prison number, her sentence, fifteen years for manslaughter in the second degree, the date she will be eligible for parole, March 15, 1993, and her maximum release date, October 12, 1995.

He then notes that she has received alcohol counseling, but adds: "You've been involved in a lot of assaults, two of which resulted in deaths, one was your son. What do you plan to do?"

Delia leans her arms on the table and speaks in a quiet, rehearsed manner.

"I plan to go to New London."

"Do you have any relatives there?"

"My goddaughter and her nineteen-year-old son."

"How do you feel about your ability to handle your alcohol problems if paroled?"

"For years I was in denial that I had a problem but I went to counseling."

"Well, you've had quite a tragic record since 1962. Seven years ago you repeated and it seems that much of it is related to alcohol. What changed your thinking?"

"The Lord."

Mangini pauses, then calls a short recess. Out in the hallway Delia cries, mostly out of relief. She is shaking and breathing hard. After the clerk announces her name again, she rises slowly, hobbles back into the room, and takes her seat. Mangini folds his arms and leans toward her to announce the board's decision.

"Given the extreme seriousness of your offenses," he says, "the propensity in the past that you've shown. . . . We don't want to eliminate the seriousness of these offenses. We commend your rehabilitative efforts, academic efforts, especially for your age. But we'd like you to come back before the board in December 1993."

The decision comes as no surprise. Even her sponsor says that perhaps given her poor health and tenuous living arrangements, it's better that she stay where things are certain and secure. Delia, too, appears to be relieved. Back in her room, she changes into her bathrobe and collapses into bed, still shaken by the experience. "I'm just glad they didn't ask me about Darryl," she says.

The next night, Delia dreams she is drifting in a small boat down a muddy river. As she approaches a bridge, she notices a young man standing in the middle waving his arms for help. Though she can barely see him through the rain, she knows it's Darryl and he's calling to her. She stands up, nearly tipping over the boat. She stretches out her hands, hoping to pull him in before passing beneath the bridge.

"I could almost touch him, feel his fingertips," Delia says while staring up at her ceiling. She wraps her arms tight around a pillow and sits at the edge of her bed recalling the dream with a sad longing. "Then the boat passes under the bridge and when I look up Darryl is gone."

8

A Life of Tragedy

At the all-black high school in Granite Quarry, North Carolina, young Delia was starring in a play about a girl named Belinda who rode a big red bicycle. It was a mild spring afternoon in 1942 and her grandfather, Daddy Ruff, sat out in the audience beaming with pride. But midway through the play, as Delia stood center stage reciting her lines, she saw the principal come through the auditorium door and pull Daddy aside. Within seconds the principal motioned her down from the stage. Without anyone saying anything, Delia knew in her heart that her mother, Cardie, who had been sick for months, had taken a turn for the worse and that she and Daddy needed to rush home.

Not yet forty, Cardie had been plagued with a series of illnesses, caused by having too many children too close together in addition to a number of miscarriages. She had worked hard to support her family by cooking in a segregated restaurant named The White Folks Cafe, and had taught Delia how to cook like a professional. Cardie always called Delia, the sixth of her seven children, her "favorite baby," and requested from her deathbed that she be by her side.

When Delia walked into her mother's bedroom, she found it jammed with aunts, uncles, neighbors, and the family's minister. They had all come to say goodbye. Making her way through the thicket of mourners, the nine-year-old girl met her mother's eyes and took hold of her hand. "Baby, don't ever go any place without telling someone where you're going," Cardie said to her second youngest, but before the little girl could nod her head, Cardie was dead.

As he had promised his daughter, Daddy Ruff continued to raise Delia and her brothers Meme and Marion in the tidy white clapboard house on Highway 52. Cardie's older children had all moved north. As the only female around, Delia reveled in her role as woman of the house. Each day after school, she would cook and clean, wash clothes in the basin out on the back porch, and make certain things were tidy for when Daddy came home from work.

Every afternoon at 4:30 she would meet him at Lyley's country store. He would drive up in his green Hudson sedan, his beard covered in rock dust and sweat. Once he saw his granddaughter he would break into a wide smile. Already old and somewhat sickly by the time his daughter died, Daddy still maintained a lean, distinguished stature that made Delia feel protected and safe. He smelled sweet and musty from the pipe tobacco he smoked, and he always tucked his thumbs under his suspenders when he spoke to her in his quiet, guiding way.

At school Delia made good grades and showed signs of becoming a leader. She felt proud that, unlike many students' parents, who were sharecroppers, Daddy was a hardworking, God-loving, teetotaling man who worked for a steady wage in the quarries. But even he could not placate the restlessness that seized the young girl by the time she reached adolescence. At fourteen, she began spending time with an older girl named Mamie Lee who loved to hang out and drink moonshine at the "piccolo joint" in the woods about a mile from Delia's home.

Situated inside an abandoned hunter's shack, the "joint" contained tables for gambling and a juke box. There was a huge still out back. One night before Daddy got home from work, Delia met Mamie Lee there and proceeded, for the first time in her life, to get howling drunk on moonshine. Sick, overcome with guilt, and fearing that Daddy would never forgive her, Delia decided not to go home that night.

The next morning her brother Marion went scouting for her, and found her resting in a pine grove in the woods behind their home. Still tipsy and fettered down with shame, Delia followed her brother back to the house where she decided to end it all by drinking a mixture of warm water and a medicine called bluestone, used to treat ailing cows. It only made her nauseated and caused her to vomit. Later, when Daddy came home from work, he took one look at her and began to cry.

To Daddy's dismay, the incident did not deter her from returning again and again to the "piccolo joint." In another incident, Delia got into a fracas with her Uncle Albert after he propositioned one of her girlfriends. "He offered the girl money and began pulling and tugging at her, just carrying on," Delia recalls from her prison room on a frigid winter morning. Full of moonshine, Delia smacked him across the face and he knocked her to the ground and kept on hitting her until someone went to get Daddy. Later, when Uncle Albert tried to visit their house, Daddy met him with a shotgun. He would not allow him inside for months.

The "piccolo joint" was also where Delia met George Strouder, a married man eleven years her senior. He became her first love and confidante and the two carried on for years. George held a steady job and tried to warn her about the dangers of alcohol, but at age fourteen, Delia would hear none of it. "If I would have listened to him, I wouldn't be in all this mess," she says nearly forty-six years later. She says she is still in love with him.

Somehow, Delia managed to keep up her schoolwork and earn top grades. Early in her senior year of high school, the principal chose her to be valedictorian and she decided to give a speech about the evils of drinking. Just then Daddy got sick with dropsy and everything seemed to fall apart. She stopped going to school so that she could take care of him and she never graduated. That summer Daddy died.

When Delia thinks about what caused her to make such a wreck out of her life and end up in a prison in southeastern Connecticut, she traces it all back to the summer she lost Daddy and the years that followed. The identity of her real father has always remained a mystery. Before her death, her mother told Delia that a Mr. "Little John" Capus from South Carolina fathered her. But after her mother died, Delia's aunts said that was a lie, and that her father was actually Daddy. Delia never believed it because of Daddy's god-fearing nature and the fact that he never tried anything on her. "God knows he could have, too," she says. "I was young and defenseless, and he could have done anything to me. But Daddy wasn't like all these men today, abusing their kids and thinking nothin' of it."

After that summer Delia traveled to Baltimore to live with her oldest sister, Myrt, her husband, Buster, and their three children. Then the six of them moved to New Haven where Delia's brothers Drip and Meme had settled. It was 1949 and Delia was sixteen. Though they did not come for the same reason, the family followed a vast migration of blacks from the deep South that began in the 1940s, when the mechanical cotton picker took the place of manual laborers. In search of economic comfort and legal rights, what many like Delia's family found instead were dreadful conditions such as those of New Haven's Oak Street, a stretch of slums resembling Harlem, which had served as the home for waves of Jewish, Irish, and Italian immigrants before them.

Delia refers to Oak Street as the Wild Wild West because of its lawlessness. The place pulsated with street brawls, public drunkenness, and a busy heroin trade. Rats as big as cats scoured the streets, prompting Mayor Richard C. Lee in the mid-1950s to implement a series of eradication programs that killed 4,000 rodents.

When they first moved to New Haven, Delia and Myrt's family all lived in one room inside Brother Meme's apartment. While the adults went out drinking and cavorting, Delia was saddled with the responsibility of babysitting. Many nights, she would sit and listen to the howls and bawls of knife fights and domestic disputes echoing through the hallways. Outside, drunks and drug dealers cluttered the sidewalks and alleyways.

One night Delia's brothers Meme, Fats, and Drip (named after a popular jitterbug song, "The Honey Dipper") got into a fight with a group of neighborhood characters; all three men ended up in the hospital with broken bones. Before long, Myrt began dragging her younger sister into "all the craziness," by taking her out drinking and meeting men.

One of her first serious romances was with Junior Robinson, a construction worker eleven years old than she, with a charm that drew women to him. The relationship lasted twenty years and Delia eventually took his last name for her own. Short and muscular, Junior was a heavy drinker and a former boxer who taught Delia how to fight by beating her until she started to strike back. Their wild drinking binges often led to boxing matches inside Junior's living room.

"Everybody liked Junior," Delia recalls. Her affection for the man is evident. She smiles widely every time she says his name. "He was funny and good-natured and gave me plenty of money," she says. Junior had another girlfriend who used to come around where Delia was living and try to beat her up. "I was no fighter at that time," she says. "But the more Junior fought me, and the more I learned how to fight him back, I could fight anybody."

When Mayor Lee began leveling the Oak Street area as part of the country's first major urban renewal effort, Delia and Junior got an apartment in the Hill. Meme and his family moved to a housing project in the Westville section, where they lived for the next thirty-eight years. Fats moved to Maryland and allegedly committed suicide by lying down on some railroad tracks, though his girlfriend suspected that he was murdered and his body later placed there. His dismembered body was returned to Granite Quarry and buried next to Cardie and Daddy Ruff. Drip developed two vocations, one as a construction worker and the other as a pimp, lining up "his girls" on Columbus Avenue. Myrt and her family moved in with a family she knew from home, Reverend Thomas and his wife, who started a storefront church on Asylum Street. Delia played the piano there on Sundays.

From the time she was a teenager until she was twenty-seven, Delia held a steady job as a cutter and presser for the May Coat Company, where she acquired several permanent scars from iron burns. She also worked as a cook's assistant at a Chinese restaurant on State Street. Her personal life, however, reflected a different side of her altogether. Out on the streets she had emerged as one of the neighborhood's toughest characters.

She was first arrested for assault in her mid-twenties, and several times thereafter, always when she had been drinking. When she was twenty-eight and still seeing Junior, she met a man named Charlie Moore and began an affair with him on the sly. The two errant lovers fought constantly. One drunken evening, in an attempt to protect herself, Delia pulled out a knife and stabbed Charlie in the chest, puncturing his lung. After spending a couple of weeks in the hospital, he left New Haven and moved back to North Carolina. Meanwhile, Delia was sentenced to nine months in the Whalley Avenue jail. It was there that she began an affair with one of the guards, Sidney Rawls. Before long, she became pregnant with Darryl.

"Once that happened he didn't want to have anything to do with me," she says about Rawls, who was married. "He denied that he was the father and I took him to court and won, proving that he was. Later a scandal broke out and he was fired for supplying women with liquor and having sex with them."

Despite the acrimony, her need for money and her child's need for a father persuaded Delia to allow Rawls to continue to be part of her life for years. Darryl adored him and pined for him every time he left their house. But apart from a destructive dependence, the relationship had little to offer her.

"That man was a smooth-talking liar," Delia says. Her expression is pure exasperation. "All he had was money, money, money. He'd do the same manipulating thing to Darryl that he'd do to me. He wrecked my life. He'd just come in and go to bed and say he was going to marry me. But he never stayed. One time he hit Darryl in the face when he was a little boy. I'll never forget that."

Things at home were complicated by Delia's drinking and volatile behavior. Seven years after she stabbed Charlie Moore, Delia was playing cards with a girlfriend of one of her brothers, with whom he had had a child. According to Delia, the woman was a prostitute and always known for starting fights. An argument broke out between the two women and Delia ended it by stabbing the woman to death.

When she came to Niantic in 1969, Darryl was seven. His aunt Myrt and uncle Meme shared his care, but for some reason that Delia does not understand to this day, they allowed the state to place him in foster care at a home in New Britain, a medium-sized town south of Hartford. Psychological testing showed that he was confused and obsessed with wanting to take care of and protect his mother. Every two weeks, prison officials would drive Delia to New Britain or Darryl would come to Niantic. They often spent weekend furloughs together.

When Delia was first admitted to the Farm, she spent several weeks in the prison's psychiatric ward for depression. Once she regained her mental strength, she started working as a kitchen assistant in the psych ward. She was able to support herself and her son by cleaning houses for prison staff and washing their cars. After a while, she got a work-release job cooking for a local nursing home called the Nutmeg Pavilion.

Delia had begun honing her cooking talents while growing up in the South, learning first from her mother and later as the young woman-of-the-house in charge of dinners and picnics for her extended family and friends. As an inmate at the Farm in the late sixties and early seventies her gifts did not go unnoticed. The COs installed a gas stove in the living room area of her cottage, Fenwick North. Delia took on the role of resident cook, planning and orchestrating sit-down dinners for inmates and staff. Nicknamed "blowouts," they often included five or six kinds of meats, vegetables, salads, and desserts, accompanied by homemade breads and several beverages. She and Bobbie Moore made turtle soup several times from a recipe of Junior Robinson's, along with fried fish and hush puppies. They concocted poke salads by scouting the lush meadows and woods, gathering wild greens and mixing them with strawberries and asparagus left from the farming days.

Eventually, Delia moved into her own room on the second floor of Fenwick North, which was considered the honors cottage, housing about twenty women. The doors were kept unlocked and there was no night supervisor. Back then the entire prison population numbered only about a hundred. Sober and without the interpersonal struggles of home, Delia's kindness and willingness to listen and give sound advice, earned her the reputation as everybody's "Ma." She also began taking classes, eventually passing the high school equivalency exam.

When Delia left the Farm in 1974, Meme drove to the prison towing a U-Haul. Along with a color television, clothes, and pots and pans, they loaded thirty-five boxes in all. Inmates and staff held a tearful goodbye banquet for her at the Nautilus Restaurant in Niantic.

Soon after arriving in New Haven, Delia rented an apartment on Howard Avenue, near City Point on the harbor, and settled in with Darryl. Advised by her social worker not to work so she could care for her son full time, she survived on welfare checks and the money she had managed to put away from her prison jobs.

About fourteen months later, Delia had some friends over and "got into a fuss" with her landlord, who lived downstairs. One thing led to another and she ended up shoving him. Before she knew it, her nephew, his girlfriend, and Junior's cousin beat him up "real bad," she says. He called the police and Delia was sent back to the Farm for nine months for violating parole. She got her old job back at the nursing home and resumed cooking her sit-down dinners for inmates and staff. Darryl, age thirteen, stayed with his godmother.

During her second go-round at the Farm, Delia says she began soul-searching for the first time in her life. She joined Alcoholics Anonymous and began to realize how her drinking had taken over and eroded her life. When she got out in 1975, she rented an apartment in New London, hoping to start a new and more constructive life. As long as she and Darryl were alone together, they got along well, she says. Nevertheless, their six-year separation had a major impact on the boy's sense of security, for which he never forgave her. He started getting into fights and as a consequence, spent time in the state's juvenile detention home in Middletown. For Delia, her son's behavior was hauntingly familiar.

"Darryl was just like me," she says. "He had this big smile and would walk into the room and everybody would want to be around him. But he also had this violent temper that ran in the family. He blamed me for a lot of his problems. Every time he would start acting crazy he'd say how I'd left him for other people to mistreat him. I think he hated me for that. But he also loved me."

About a year after she got out of prison, some friends from New Haven dropped by and introduced Delia to Charlie Gorham. It was a fortuitous meeting.

"They called Charlie 'the old man,' Delia recalls. Somehow we were having fun sitting around the kitchen table and I ended up on the old man's lap. Don't ask me what happened but when they were ready to return to New Haven that night I jumped up and said, 'Go ahead, but the old man is staying here with me'—and he did.

"He had a job in New Haven and he was commuting back and forth every day by Amtrak until someone who had an asphalt company in New London gave him a job. Darryl loved him and started calling him 'Pop' right away. I guess the boy was getting tired of babysitting me. He was fourteen then."

Within the next two years, Darryl started taking drugs and drinking. He continued to get into fights. When he was not drinking, Delia said they had many good times together, talking, cooking, and watching television programs such as All-star Wrestling. But his verbal and physical abuse toward his mother continued to escalate. Several times he beat her and bruised her and told her he wanted to kill her. After the incident at the family Fourth of July picnic, when he pummeled her face so badly that her eyes were swollen shut for days, Delia decided to enlist her son in the navy in the hopes it might straighten him out. For three years it appeared that the regimen had helped, but when he got out at age twenty, Darryl's alcohol problems returned along with his venomous behavior. After he nearly beat Charlie Gorham to death with an ashtray stand, he continued to terrorize his mother, who never filed a criminal complaint against him.

The night of his death, Darryl was drunk and had come home early. According to court testimony, Delia called a friend, Elizabeth Wongus, around 10:30 or 11:00, sounding frightened and in need of help. She then called the police, asking them to get her son out of the house. But they did not arrive soon enough to prevent what her lawyer called "the inevitable." As the evening wore on, Darryl became more and more enraged, telling his mother and her husband that he planned to kill them. Once he began beating her, Delia panicked and picked up a kitchen knife and fatally stabbed him. He was her only child, the same person, wrote her lawyer, "who had returned her love and care with humiliation, brutality and torment for so long."

Eight years later, as she stretches out on her prison bed clutching an afghan, Delia looks back at her life and wonders how different things might have been had her mother lived, and had she known her father. She recalls that as a young woman she went through a period of promiscuity with men who she knew were only using her, but that her craving for affection often overrode her better judgment. Without a doubt, she adds, alcohol helped to fuel her delusions about love.

Without the support and guidance she has received from her family at the Farm, she feels she would have died or gone into a self-destructive tailspin years ago. Since her incarceration began in 1985, she has undergone extensive counseling for her alcoholism and behavior problems, and has tried to help countless inmates come to grips with similar problems.

As the months pass since her first attempt to make parole, Delia has begun to mention Darryl's name on a casual basis more and more, as if she has finally managed to put the pain of the experience into a separate, guarded place. She tells the story of how, when Darryl was just a baby, she and Junior took him to North Carolina, where the couple spent several months working on a tobacco farm as sharecroppers. The owner, a Mr. Clarke, gave her a horse to plow the fields with, but soon discovered that her kitchen skills were much more valuable to his family and work crew. So while the men labored under the hot sun, Delia, with Darryl by her side, worked in the house where the heat was much more tolerable. Those were the happy times.

When she does speak about Darryl's death, she often says that her son was as much a victim of her alcoholism and volatile actions as she was of her own misguided life, influenced by friends and relatives whom she could hardly call role models. "Everything that happened in my life pretty much led to that night," she says, early one morning. "Darryl always knew what would happen if he fought me for too long. Maybe if I hadn't been drinking that night none of this would've happened. But I was this crazy alcoholic mother and he had all those problems, too. In the end, it was either him or me."

PART

2

"This isn't a prison for criminals, it's a prison for drug addicts."

—Dawn, an inmate

9

The Baker House Pioneers

Since her arrival in the spring of 1992, Dunn has been working hard to fulfill her dream of opening the prison system's first residential drug treatment program. The project is several months ahead of schedule. Lucretia Shaw, one of the original cottages, has been partially renovated and contains room for thirty-two inmates. The building will serve as the program's first home. At the end of a tree-lined path, it is the most isolated spot on the prison grounds with the most beautiful views of the lake and woods. Inside the sun-filled bunk room, the walls are freshly painted with natural tones and the tiled floors have a silky gloss. There is a spacious dining and television room with a big screen and private offices for counseling. Throughout September, drug counselors have canvassed the cottages and York dormitory to solicit volunteers. By the end of September, the first participants settle in.

The rehabilitation project is named after a former inmate and drug addict, Marilyn Baker, who died in 1991 at the age of fifty-one. The product of a tumultuous home life, she began experimenting with drugs as a teenager, which led to a succession of arrests and prison terms. She was eventually forced to give up her children to foster care. But each time she left the prison, those who knew her say she was determined to change. In 1986, she started nursing school and completed training as a drug-abuse counselor. Two years later, Baker was hired as a counselor at the women's prison and introduced several programs. But by then she had become ill with an aggressive form of cancer, which gradually forced her to use crutches, and later, a wheelchair. Despite the obstacles, Baker worked tirelessly with inmates to help them break the cycle of drugs and crime.

Only a few weeks have passed since the Baker House opened and the mood is shaky. Kathy Mayer, the program's director, notes that the urgency in having to fill the beds to ease the prison's congestion has left little time to prepare a screening plan. Women are allowed in with severe mental health problems; others come in ill because they are detoxifying from drugs. Several women have HIV. Most participants come from backgrounds full of sexual, physical, and emotional abuse as well as family histories of drug and alcohol addiction. It is suspected that one of the participants is the president of the prison's Latin Queens, which might intimidate the others and keep them from speaking frankly about their problems.

A typical participant, Margy Hernandez has mixed her drug addiction with prostitution. On a nippy fall day, she tells me her story while we sit on a picnic bench facing the lake. Her sentences pour out in swift strokes, frequently cut short in a clipped English. She has shoulder-length, coal black hair, and a round, animated face. The reasons she gives for working the streets are the same as those of other inmates in the program. She loves the theatrics of dressing up like a movie star, wearing black high heels, and painting on cat-eyes, then going out on the stroll and having everyone stare. There is the irresistible taboo of living on the dark side and the thrill of meeting men from all walks of life (Polish men are the cheapest, she tells me, Italians are big spenders). She always has her own money and plenty of it.

Margy came to Niantic on larceny and theft charges. "I love to steal Cadillacs," she squeals. She rambles through the peaks of her life, dressing it with hyperbole. She has two children. Her father and brother are addicts and alcoholics. She's a Latin Queen and her sister is a twenty-two-year-old pediatrician. "I used to be a compulsive liar," she says, "but since I've been in the program I've seen a lot of changes."

It all started in the summer of 1984. Margy was walking down a busy street on the east side of Bridgeport when a man in a limousine swooped to the curb next to her and asked if she wanted a ride. At first she resisted but she finally got in. They drove a few blocks before he leaned over and put his hand on her knee. Margy, then seventeen, thought, hmmmm, now what? "Finally," she says to me, "this guy says he'll give me a hundred dollars for a blow job and I think, Wow, that's all I have to do is give him a blow job and he'll give me a hundred dollars?" Apparently, the offer was too good to refuse.

A few years later as she strolled the Washington Park area in Bridgeport trying to pick up the wealthier clientele from the Fairfield County suburbs, Margy spotted a white man in a silver Rolls Royce who motioned to her to get into his car. By then, she had designed her own illusive aura of seduction. "I looked real good that night," she says. "I had on a short, tight black dress, that made my butt look big and my waist real thin." They ended up in a hotel room in Fairfield and began to party. Margy introduced the man to crack, and like many first-time users, she says, "he began to bug, to get afraid." She told him that before she could have sex, she needed more crack and that they would have to go back to Bridgeport to buy some. Too paranoid to leave the room, the man gave Margy the keys to his car. It was the last he saw of his silver Rolls Royce.

"I took the keys, got into the car and drove off to find my friend Willie. We brought it into this garage and stripped the whole motherfuckin' thing, then went out and sold the parts. And that's how it started. I'd pick up some rich trick, get him high, then steal his keys and go find Willie. A lot of times Willie used to wait for me outside motel rooms. We made big-time money in those days."

A few minutes later, Margy, dressed in baggy sweat pants, no make-up, and a V-necked T-shirt, stands in front of a circle of inmates and sings a capella Whitney Houston's song, "He Builds Me Up." She changes the lyrics by substituting the male pronoun with the name of God. Her voice is clear and flawless, but a little shaky on the high notes. "God gives me hope, He gives me love, more, more than I'll ever know," she wails as her cottagemates break into applause. Some wipe away tears.

The Baker House program is based on a combination of behavior modification and twelve-step principles that originated with Alcoholics Anonymous. Daily morning meetings such as these aim to inspire inmates and chisel away the mistrust innate in the prison culture. As a member of the first group of inmates to enter the program, Margy is considered one of its pioneers. She and her thirty-one housemates have been given the opportunity to shape its direction by forming committees, devising house rules, and handling discipline problems. They begin their day by gathering in the dining room to sing, read inspirational passages, share experiences, and dance. The rest of the day is filled with classes and therapy sessions. Watching television is limited to certain hours. Instead, the women spend most of their free time reading, writing in their journals, or working on creative projects. They are not allowed to go to Monday night socials, to school, or to walk the grounds, and they cannot mix with the outside prison population. Several times a week some receive acupuncture treatments to reduce cravings for drugs or alcohol. Within the first few weeks, one resident writes the Marilyn Baker House credo. Another resident stencils it on the wall of the meeting room. Both women ask to remain anonymous.

> Within these walls stand courageous women
> who have become dedicated to
> the belief that there is no gain without pain;
> That to endure life we must struggle to meet
> challenges and stand tall and proud in the
> face of our own worse enemy.
>
> We have come to accept that with determination
> and commitment to our common goal of becoming
> drug-free, we will find meaning and worth in
> ourselves and ultimately, peace and tranquility.
>
> Therefore: if you treat a woman as she is, she
> will stay as she is, but if you treat her as she ought
> to be and could be, she will become as she ought to
> be and could be. . . . . and more.

Initially just a handful of women speak out in group therapy sessions, but within a few weeks women who have never shared their stories begin opening up. Like Margy, many of the women have been in and out of Niantic too many times to count. Many have given up children for adoption, or to foster care or relatives, and carry only memories and perhaps a child's photograph.

Often the group therapy discussions revolve around relationships and children. One morning an inmate named Sarah begins by saying she is upset because she wants to break up with her girlfriend who is still doing drugs. The women sit in a large circle with sunlight pouring in from windows at each end of the room. A refrigerator sits in one corner. The meeting is a breakthrough, in that more than just a few residents toss glimpses of themselves into the pool of discussion.

Toni: Sarah, you've got to think about yourself, you can't worry about someone else. I have the same problems with the man I'm with. The thing is, some partners are just bad news.

Sonya: I know love is strong, Sarah, but this disease is too. It's real powerful and you have to put everything into recovery.

Jan: It's hard though, when you know your kids are out there without you. I was supposed to receive a visit from my kids, but it got canceled. I haven't seen them in a month.

Margy: I've seen my daughter but I haven't seen my son because he lives with my aunt and she keeps him away from me. Sometimes I'll be sitting on my bed just staring at my son's pictures, I'll be staring into them. But who are we fooling? When we were in the streets we didn't drop a tear when someone said, Let me take your baby for a week. Oh sure, we'd say, take them, 'cause we were too high to deal with them.

Tanya: Out of ten years, I've seen my son three times. My father raised him.

Patty: I have an eight and a nine-year-old and I've hardly seen them at all.

Sonya: When we get visits you want to overwhelm them with love because of all the guilt and shame you feel. And that's the same guilt that gets you down and drives you out there to do drugs.

Toni: Sonya, you shouldn't feel so much guilt now because you're in here doing good for yourself and your kids.

Ellen: When I was twenty-eight, I left my husband and kids because of alcohol. Twenty-two years later I saw my daughter and we visited for about three hours. She has a baby and she told me that every time she looked at her baby she'd say to herself, How could my mother leave me? After we saw each other I got into trouble and everything fell apart. I haven't seen my daughter since, but I'm grateful for the time we were able to spend together.

Tanya: I worry about my kids. I worry that all I'll ever be able to do is prostitute because that's all I've ever done. Fast money leads you to do drugs and pull tricks.

Ellen: But Tanya, I've seen so many changes in you. It is possible to change.

Ellen Marks, fifty-two years old, was a close friend and client of Marilyn Baker. She often talks to the residents in the rehabilitation program about how Baker inspired everyone with her laughter and common sense, and how they all owe it to her memory to shed the dead-end behaviors of their pasts. Almost immediately, Marks becomes an anchor for the program and some of the women start calling her Grandma, a name that sticks. Inmates are drawn by her vitality and middle-class stability, which conceals a strong rebelliousness she has worked hard to control.

After one group meeting she tells me about her past. We are sitting in the dining hall and she wears a peach-colored chiffon blouse with black pants. Her silver-blond hair is bobbed and she wears blue framed glasses, which give her a bohemian flair. It is easy to see why younger inmates cling to her. She has a soft, whimsical side to her character that has probably helped her negotiate through the jolts and currents of her life.

She comes from an alcoholic family, and her mother committed suicide. After she left her husband and three children at the age of twenty-eight, she worked in bars and "lived a fast life that I never considered as right or wrong." In 1979, she stopped drinking, joined Alcoholics Anonymous, and for nine years remained sober, working as a receptionist for a tax preparer in Boston. "Then I met this guy who liked to party and we got involved. Turns out he's an alcoholic and heroin addict with a three-hundred-dollar a day habit. After I met him I felt my life go out of control."

Soon after, Marks stopped going to AA meetings and was laid off from her job. To support her boyfriend's habit, the couple went on a spree through Connecticut, Massachusetts, New York, and Rhode Island that included twenty-one robberies, mostly of video stores, gourmet shops, and boutiques. "We didn't hurt or kill anybody," she says. She received a sentence of twenty-two and a half years in Niantic with no parole. Marks had no other police record. "I think the judge was biased because it was the fiftieth anniversary of the death of Bonnie and Clyde." She takes a slow drag off a generic cigarette. "He hated my boyfriend. In court he told me, 'Lady, you met yourself a real asshole.' "

I am reminded of what Donna Henry, a drug counselor at Niantic, told me a few weeks before about the reasons prisoners give for their actions. Henry had counseled both male and female inmates. "When you're talking to men they often say, 'Man, if I could just find myself a good woman.' Whereas, the women will tell you, 'Man, if I could just get rid of that asshole.' " The Baker House residents express similar sentiments.

Marks still has to serve time in Massachusetts and the other states, but she hopes the state of Connecticut can strike a compromise which will enable her to serve most of her sentence in Niantic. To keep her mind off her problems, she spends her free time playing Yahtzee with Patty Stoltz, an intense, introspective woman who has been a prostitute and a drug addict since the age of eleven.

At thirty-four, Patty has been in an out of Niantic about twenty-nine times, she says, mostly on drug charges. She has contracted the AIDS virus, but unlike other inmates with the disease, she speaks out about it and how it has affected her physically and emotionally. She has lost many teeth to cocaine and poor health care, but she has clear blue eyes and a rosy complexion. She dresses mostly in sporty sweat suits. She does not possess Ellen's sympathetic nature, but she is respected for her insights and street-wise soul.

Patty claims that because of drugs and a learning disability, she has a poor memory and finds it difficult to understand when someone speaks quickly, or uses big words. Married twice, both times to men from Colombia, she has a basic comprehension of Spanish and resents it when the Puerto Rican women in the program speak about the others in a catty manner. One morning, Patty and Margy argue about housekeeping chores, and Margy stomps off mumbling something in Spanish. The tension between the two women has been building since the beginning of the program, and for Patty, this is the last straw. She complains to the counselors that Margy gossips about her in Spanish. She wants the matter discussed in a private but supervised meeting.

The counselors, E. J. Johnson and Liz Martinez, agree, and they call Patty and Margy together in the television room one afternoon. Patty begins the conversation by looking directly at Margy and saying, "Look Margy, I don't know everything that you're saying but I can pick up enough words to know that you're talking about me and what's happening." Margy stares at the floor for several minutes. She has an anxious and angry look on her face. Finally she says, "Look, I have a lot of problems that I can't tell anybody about. I wish everyone would just leave me alone." Martinez tells Margy how her behavior is causing pain and disrupting the program. Margy wraps her arms tightly around her chest and keeps her mouth clamped.

Later all the residents gather to discuss the issue. They agree that it is divisive to talk about someone in a language they do not understand, and so is making fun of someone's accent or pronunciation. In the future, they decide, neither behavior will be tolerated.

Over the next few weeks, Margy grows more and more moody and withdraws, lying on her bed most of the day. She tells me she thinks all the open discussions are phony and that people should stay out of her business.

For Halloween, residents make a spoof out of prison life by dressing up as hookers, correction officers, prisoners in handcuffs, and witches. They dance to rap and Latin music, dunk for apples, and play "stick" the tail on the donkey (pins would be considered contraband).

Despite the good feelings evident at the party, below the surface roils a current of cynicism. Margy and a number of other inmates agree that the program is all for show and chock full of con artists. Some people who smile, tell their stories, and pledge to get sober, then sneak in drugs and get high. In the weeks that follow, one woman is thrown out of the program after her urine test for drugs shows up positive. Another, who has served her time and leaves to enroll in a drug program in Hartford, tells me, "I'm just thankful to get away from all these hypocrites." Within the weeks that follow, Margy leaves voluntarily and moves into York dormitory, also known as Calcutta.

Most of the women, however, say they are desperate to stay clean, and they see completing the program as a major milestone. Cassandra Palmer hopes the Marilyn Baker House will save what is left of her life. She came into the program detoxifying from heroin and ill from HIV. "I felt sick and lousy," she says a few days into November. "I was pissed off and didn't care what anybody said. I had the fuck-ups real bad."

Cassandra has worked in massage parlors, among other places, and once appeared on the Geraldo Rivera Show in a segment about street prostitutes. One shot showed her in a crack house cooking dope.

After a few weeks at the Baker House she begins to feel better. She speaks out in meetings and befriends many of the women, who appreciate her maternal tone. She calls everyone "hon." She has an outspoken, sometimes macabre sense of humor. If she has extra food or cigarettes she makes "goody bags" for inmates in need.

The residents of the program are encouraged to keep journals and to write their life history, an exercise Cassandra warms to. In an eight-page, hand-written essay, she tells about growing up with a mentally ill mother and physically abusive grandmother.

"I guess I would start from the time my father was deported back to Spain," the letter begins, "my grandma told me that she had him deported because he was perverted that he did sexual things to me that I wouldn't remember because I was to young, and I always felt like this was my fault"

She goes on to write about how she became a ward of the state at age twelve when her grandmother died. The state had a difficult time placing her in a foster home because of her age, and placed her for two years in the Connecticut Valley Hospital in Middletown, where she was anesthetized with high doses of thorazine.

Well there was all kinds of women in this place one of them use to strip her clothes and piss from chair to chair another one had lost her child in a car accident so she use to sit in a corner talking to this rabbit as if it were her child I remember feeling sorry for her. And I'll never forget the lady who use to like to pull you by the back of your head and she wouldn't let loose she grabbed me one time about a month after I got there when I tried to defend myself I was thrown on the ground by the staff there and given a extra dose of thorazine injected by a needle in my but then they put me in a bed and wrapped me tight in sheets and I remember thinking God what did I do to deserve this Please help me but he didn't well the medication was so strong I fell out I don't remember for how long but when I woke up I was still wrapped in sheets eventually they did let me get up for dinner but first I was put in a straight jacket and one of the nurses fed me. I eventually got to actually like to be here I felt like this is where I belonged it was better then being beaten and humiliated then again it wasn't any better there but to me it was. Well as time went on I started acting like the people there I started rocking a lot till this day I catch myself still doing it at times when I'm nervous and I also went on to be very suicidal I started cutting my wrists and then when they would stick up my arms I would pull the stitches out because I felt that I deserved the pain and eventually grew to like this.

After Connecticut Valley, Cassandra was transferred to the Long Lane Reformatory, also in Middletown, where she spent the rest of her adolescence. At eighteen, she married a man who beat her frequently. The couple had two children and divorced three years later.

On the way to see the prison psychiatrist one blustery November day, Cassandra says she feels tired all the time, because her T-cell count has dropped below two hundred. Her thick brown hair streaked with premature silver whips away from her drawn face. Her hazel eyes are speckled with green. She doesn't know whether she can keep up the emotional momentum needed to succeed in the program, and wishes she could go home to her family on the streets. She especially misses her friend Chris, a gay man and an addict with AIDS. "It all makes me want to get out of this hellhole and go back to the streets to die," she says, quickly catching herself. "I know that's a death wish. I know staying in this program is the best thing for me."

In Niantic, inmates receive discipline for displaying sexual affection. Such actions at the Marilyn Baker House result in expulsion from the program. One evening while the residents relax and watch a Michael Jackson television special, two women known to be sexually involved embrace while sitting on the couch. One resident gets up and tells the correction officer on duty. Several days later, Kathy Mayer calls the residents to a meeting where she confronts several women about rumors that they have violated sexual conduct rules. While the couple who had been on the couch a few evenings before deny any wrongdoing, two other women admit they have been intimate. Both are expelled from the program.

Cassandra, who has been friends with the two women, is devastated. The day after their dismissal, she confronts the inmate who had reported the couch incident and shouts in her face, "You don't go snitching on somebody's relationship!" Stunned, the woman turns and races out of the room. Cassandra, with her fists clenched, follows her to her bunk and continues yelling at her. COs quickly defuse the situation. The next day, Cassandra is expelled from the program and sent to Calcutta.

By the end of December, ten of the women have either left the Marilyn Baker House voluntarily or been expelled, leaving the mood in the cottage somber and introspective.

A few weeks after Cassandra leaves the program, an inmate named Tanya is expelled for assault. It is another case in which many of the residents feel that the woman deserves a second chance. Mayer calls a group meeting a few days later, at which she admonishes some of the residents for perpetuating acrimony and spreading the details of the program's problems to the outside prison population. Sitting at the head of the room, in a conservative gray-blue suit, Mayer appears exasperated. She has run a similar program at a women's prison in Georgia, and she knows that inmates in recovery often exhibit anger and misdirected emotions. Still, she aims to make it clear that the program has no room for disruptive people. Leaning

The Evolution of a Prison

In its early years, the Connecticut Farm for Women ran one of the most efficient dairy barns in the state. The selling of dairy products as well as vegetables and fruits enabled the prison farm to become self-sufficient. In this photograph, taken in 1923, inmates stand outside the barn displaying milking canisters and pails. (Courtesy of Niantic Correctional Institution)

New Building Group Recently Added to Connecticut State Farm for Women at East Lyme

A $1,000,000 Institution—One of the Most Modern of Its Kind—With Superintendent Elizabeth Munger In Charge of 165 Women Inmates. These Additions, Together With Original Buildings, Are Scattered Over 350-acre Hillside Overlooking Bride Lake.

THE PRISON BUILDING—Among the inmates to be imprisoned in this modern building of the new group will be the women inmates of the Connecticut State Prison, who are to be transferred to this new building.

THE ADMINISTRATION BUILDING, with offices for the reception of inmates and general executive work.

THE CHIEF IN CHARGE OF THE STATE FARM FOR WOMEN — Miss Elizabeth Munger, superintendent of the Connecticut State Farm for Women.
(C) Green Jack Turner

THE INDUSTRIAL BUILDING—Containing the work

In 1930, the *Hartford Courant* featured a pictorial of the prison, showing its expansion under the supervision of Elizabeth Munger. A nationally recognized penologist, Munger had been in the forefront of the women's reformatory movement. As the Farm's superintendent, she initiated programs aimed at changing inmate behavior by teaching constructive living skills.

Inmates preparing the soil in the spring . . .

and harvesting onions in the fall during the 1930s. (Courtesy of Niantic Correctional Institution)

Inmates making croquettes during a cooking class. In addition to farming, the women at Niantic were taught domestic skills. After their release from prison, many went on to become maids or housekeepers. (Courtesy of Niantic Correctional Institution)

For decades, the prison provided its own nursery where infants of inmates sometimes lived until they were two. (Courtesy of Niantic Correctional Institution)

Two inmates enjoying a quiet moment on the shore of Bride Lake in the 1940s. Since the prison opened, the seventy-three-acre preserve has served as the setting for weddings as well as fishing and swimming outings. (Courtesy of Niantic Correctional Institution)

Inmates of earlier decades were assigned to single rooms and allowed to embellish their surroundings with curtains, skirtings, and other personal touches. In this photograph from the 1940s, an inmate confers with a prison matron during what seems to be a private tutorial. (Courtesy of Niantic Correctional Institution)

An inmate inside her cottage bedroom during the 1940s. (Courtesy of Niantic Correctional Institution)

An inmate sewing circle of the 1940s. To this day, embroidery, knitting, and crocheting serve as popular pastimes for women prisoners at Niantic. Needlework and other crafts are sent to relatives, sold at prison craft fairs, or given to sick children in need. (Courtesy of Niantic Correctional Institution)

By the 1960s, the Farm had entered a new phase under Warden Janet York. In 1966 the prison was featured in a nationally distributed Sunday newspaper supplement that lauded the facility for its low recidivism rate and innovative reform programs. The accompanying article was subtitled "The Prison that Cures by Kindness." (Courtesy of Janet York)

Prison with a View

At Niantic, Connecticut,
far-seeing jailers treat the women inmates
as individuals rather than numbers

The entrance to the Niantic Correctional Institution in the early 1990s. Throughout its history, the prison's total population had remained relatively steady. Beginning in the 1980s with the advent of crack cocaine and stricter enforcement of drug laws, Niantic's numbers soared. Gang activity and violence increased and the overall mood in corrections toward rehabilitation as a way to reduce criminal behavior began to sour. (Andrea Hoy Hansen/*The Day*)

STATE OF CONNECTICUT

DEPARTMENT OF CORRECTION
CONNECTICUT
CORRECTIONAL
INSTITUTION
NIANTIC

A 1992 view of "The Park" inside the dormitory inmates dubbed "Calcutta" because of its overcrowding, drug activity, and assaults. (Bruce Johnson/NYT Pictures)

In 1992 the prison created a gardening program to give idle inmates something constructive to do. Here two inmates pot plants inside one of the prison's greenhouses. (Bruce Johnson/NYT Pictures)

An inmate proudly displays pictures of her children. There are about 56,000 children in the United States whose mothers are incarcerated. Most, like this woman, are imprisoned for crimes related to drug addiction. (Andrea Hoy Hansen/*The Day*)

The first graduates of the Marilyn Baker House drug rehabilitation program wave good-bye to relatives after the ceremonies. (Judith Pszenica/NYT Pictures)

Beatrice Codianni-Robles surrounded by Latin Kings and Queens giving their gang salute in New Haven. Ms. Codianni-Robles was the lifeline for many Latin Queens in Niantic. She was arrested in 1994 on racketeering charges and is now serving a seventeen-year sentence in a federal prison. (David C. LaBianca/NYT Pictures)

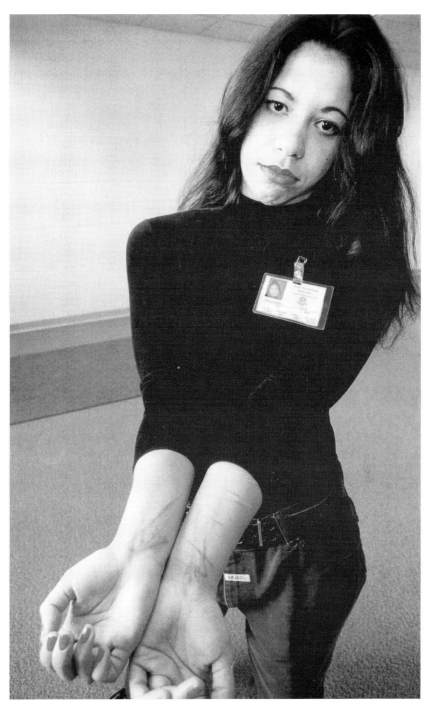

A maximum-security inmate, serving a sentence of forty years, displays scars from a suicide attempt. At age seventeen she and other members of the Los Solidos gang, a rival of the Latin Kings, stabbed to death a twenty-two-year-old woman. (Skip Weisenberger/*The Day*)

As the prison becomes more overcrowded, officials are forced to bus inmates to other prisons and turn storage rooms and the gymnasium into makeshift dormitories. Here an inmate sits on her bunk in a corroded basement annex. (Robert Patterson/*The Day*)

Another view of the "numbers crunch." (Robert Patterson/*The Day*)

A 1992 photograph of the construction of the new maximum-security facility at Niantic, built at a cost of $55 million. The stark design reflects the shift from the decades-old rehabilitation model of prison architecture to the so-called confinement model now being adopted nationwide. (Skip Weisenberger/*The Day*)

Architectural photographs of the new prison at Niantic, the Janet S. York Correctional Institution. Politicians and some staff complain that the buildings are too extravagant for prisoners and that the money spent should have gone to building schools. Other staff are relieved that the overcrowding problems have been eased, at least for the time being. (Courtesy Mark Trew/Henderson, Durham & Richardson, Inc.)

Interior views of the cafeteria . . .

and a lounge area at the new York facility. (Courtesy Mark Trew/Henderson, Durham & Richardson, Inc.)

The York prison opens in October 1994. Guests leave the reception as inmates gaze out from their dormitory windows. (Skip Weisenberger/*The Day*)

An inmate from York prison serving her third sentence at Niantic on drug-related charges. Her parents had served time in prison, as did an older brother. The occurrence of more than one generation of members of the same family serving prison time has become common throughout the United States. (Andrea Hoy Hansen/ *The Day*)

Bonnie Foreshaw inside Fenwick South. For years she has sought to appeal her forty-five-year prison sentence for murdering a pregnant woman. Claiming she was the victim of gender and race bias in the court system, she has attracted the attention of filmmakers, philanthropists, and a Connecticut attorney who has worked for years to have the case retried. (Judith Pszenica/NYT Pictures)

forward in her chair, she shifts her eyes to the twenty-some women circled around her and takes a deep breath. "You've got to get a grip," she tells the women. "Don't keep stirring things up. Talk about it in group. Because, what happens is that the focus gets moved away from the program. I know there are women who are angry that Tanya is in segregation, but I'm warning the pack leaders who keep inflaming the issues that if they continue they'll have to leave. The word is getting around the institution that there are problems here, and it looks bad on all of us."

After the meeting, the residents return to their bunks for thirty minutes of meditation and relaxation exercises. Justina Jackson, who has been diagnosed with multiple personality disorder, curls up in a corner bottom bunk and looks out a window facing Bride Lake. She hums a song she wrote about how the program has inspired her to change. As the twilight settles in the long narrow room, Justina stares out the window and smiles. She has managed to make it through the last several weeks by relying on her other selves for guidance and comfort. She loves to read in the moonlight.

Mayer turns on a tape of New Age music which floats through the cottage. Justina clutches her pillow and watches a flock of grackles blacken a russet sky. "Hmmmm, just look at this," she says dreamily, her eyes following the pattern of the birds disappearing over the horizon. "All those people out there would pay a million dollars for this view."

10

Cassandra in Calcutta

A shipment of drugs is due into York Dormitory, a.k.a., Calcutta, sometime on Friday. Cassandra expects the usual: speed, p-dope, and maybe some marijuana, which will have to be smoked in the recreation yard. Something usually comes in every weekend, either through the Visitors' Center, or from inmates returning from furloughs. Sometimes the supplier will stuff the drug into a balloon and swallow it, then take a mouthful of laxatives. Twelve hours later, voila! Double, maybe triple the street price and you can make some good money.

"There's never any works," Cassandra says, meaning syringes. "I could give a shit. I haven't gotten high since I've been here." She is sitting in the commons area that separates York North from York South, feeling lousy. Ever since she got thrown out of the Marilyn Baker House for "going off" on another inmate, Cassandra has slipped into a dark mood and "has the fucks-ups real bad." Inmates at the Baker House are upset over the whole ordeal, particularly because Cassandra is sick and has ended up back in Calcutta. While the Baker House resettles after the December shake-down, I decide to visit her in the place called Niantic's equivalent of hell. The contrast between the two worlds is wicked.

Cassandra tells me that when she first arrived here, she spent three nights sleeping on a mattress on the floor in the commons, because no beds were available. It was bad enough getting kicked out of the drug program just when her T-cell count was sinking below two hundred, she says, but getting shipped to Calcutta has really been a bruiser.

At the Baker House she had to deal with thirty-one women, and on the south side of Calcutta there are about 110, mostly unsentenced, and at least that many more on the north side. The only thing separating the two dormitories is the commons area, where Cassandra comes to socialize and forget her pain.

She is wearing a pastel sweat suit and looks bloated. The Styrofoam cup in front of her has twelve tablespoons of sugar in it. She lives on coffee and sweets. Every week one of her "tricks," a sixty-eight-year-old man, sends her forty dollars so she can get candy bars and cookies from commissary. Sometimes she has enough left over to make "goody bags" for her three cubicle mates. One, a tall black woman in an orange sweat suit, sails past us, winks at me, and says, "That's my girl you're talkin' to," and Cassandra laughs. She has a mouthful of bad teeth but her hazel eyes still hold a warm sparkle.

After three nights, Cassandra finally got a bed on the south side, a large room where inmates are assigned by fours or eights to eight-foot-square cubicles. The din of voices and commotion never ceases. It has taken about three weeks for Cassandra to learn to sleep amidst the cacophony and maneuverings, which resembles those of the streets. Somebody is always hustling something, cigarettes, candy, dope, sex. Inside Cassandra's cubicle the women have covered the wall with posters of barely clad men with bulging pectoral muscles, and photos of their children, spouses, or boyfriends. Other cubicles feature similar decor.

At the front of the room a sign reads "NO TENTS." It refers to the practice of draping sheets from the top bunk to create a private space below. The COs will tell you that a lot of women in here get pressured into having sex with the more experienced and manipulative inmates, and outlawing tents helps to curb those behaviors.

Cassandra's cubicle is catty-corner from the Park, an area with couches and a television set that blasts soap operas all afternoon. The space is always crowded with women braiding each other's hair, crocheting, chatting, or, watching a T.V. "passion play."

Across from the Park is the omnipotent Bubble, a glassed-in watchtower for the COs. Sitting inside, you feel like you are within a honeycomb swarming with obstinate bees. All day long, inmates tap on the windows asking for tampons, hair dryers, curling irons, aspirin, and other things, while COs fill requests, answer phones, record hourly counts, and monitor the inmates' activities.

And all day long COs bark commands at inmates. "Ladies, the television is supposed to be off"; "Excuse me Rivera, no more than two people on a bunk"; or "What are you doing Miss Harris? You're supposed to be confined to your quarters." The guards come out on the floor if there are fights or suspicious actions. Between the intercom, the television, and the constant chatter, many of the inmates wear headphones so they can hear themselves think.

If an inmate starts to come on to a CO, through love letters or through verbal or physical overtures, COs are supposed to report it to the warden immediately. Lt. Anthony Colonus, the man in charge of York Dormitory and a seasoned guard, advises young male COs in particular not to sit on an inmate's bed or do anything with an inmate that might be misconstrued. Inmates will frequently report any wrongdoing, legitimate or not, regardless of whether it's directed toward them or another inmate. The lieutenant knows more than one CO who has been fired for getting involved with an inmate and when it comes to a dormitory as crowded as Calcutta, the chances of that happening intensify.

Cassandra and the lieutenant have a good rapport. He tries to get jobs for as many inmates as he can, anything to keep them occupied, even if it is sorting Q-Tips for state mental institutions. Right now, he is trying to find something for Cassandra. Each week he hands out about fifty disciplines, resulting from conduct such as assaults and conducting gang activities. He used to send an inmate to segregation when she broke the rules, but like every place else, the unit is almost always on overfill. Therefore, when Colonus gives out a discipline it usually means an inmate is confined to her cubicle for a certain length of time. "If you're gonna go to jail now's the time," he once quipped to me, referring to the early release of inmates due to overcrowding.

Cassandra likes his sense of humor and calls him "a real sweetheart, a real fair egg." He gives her cigarettes in exchange for the work she does. "I don't know how he deals with all these crazy women," she says, watching him write up a discipline on an inmate who had talked out loud in the middle of the night. She turns away and pulls out a picture of her ex-boyfriend who has "turned" gay. He is sitting on a chaise longue on a beach in California, posing like a

Playgirl magazine centerfold. Cassandra took his last name but was never married to him.

After she got out of the mental hospital at age eighteen, Cassandra married a man who beat her. Three years and two children later, she left him. She met a man soon after who helped support her and get her back on her feet. After he got her best friend pregnant, Cassandra ended the relationship. She attended a secretarial school for a while, and from there got a job as a credit manager at a BP gas station in Hartford. That is where she met Eddie, the man in the photograph.

"He was beautiful, dark, and a real gentlemen," Cassandra says. "Could charm the pants off anybody." For the first time in her life she had fallen in love. Eddie took care of her kids as though they were his own. He wanted more, but Cassandra had gotten her tubes tied before she left her husband. "That really bothered Eddie," she says.

Long before she met Eddie, Cassandra started working in massage parlors. Although she never told him, she continued the practice after they met. She had this routine. Every morning Eddie dropped her off at an office building where she was supposedly doing clerical work. Once she got out of the car, she waited for Eddie to drive off and then walked a few blocks to The House of Foxes. There she assumed the identity of Loni.

She started "working parlors" because the money was good ("It was great because you could score forty to fifty dollars for a hand job, seventy to a hundred for a blow job. In the streets it's about half of that.") She also met a lot of nice guys who treated her better than some of the guys she had known on the streets. "But I had my share of weirdos too," she says, like the ones that wanted the women to beat them up and humiliate them. "One guy dressed up in a teddy and put on a dog chain and wanted to be led around on his knees. So one of us would pull him around and some other women would kick him and scream foul language at him and he loved it." Cassandra shakes her head and giggles. "Massage parlors do a real service for women because they take care of all the perverts. And those are the ones that pay the highest, anything to do with dominance."

As Cassandra had suspected, Eddie too was living in his own hidden world. "I thought for a long time he was gay but denied it to myself," she says. "But even though we had our secret lives, we also had a lot of love for each other."

When Eddie found out about the massage parlor, he packed up his things and moved to San Francisco. "After he left I started doing cocaine. I ended up homeless, because the massage parlor found out I was doing drugs and that's a no-no. I started working the streets, slept in hospitals, laundromats, abandoned houses. One night I got into the car with this white guy, a real all-American type. He tied me up with rope and tape, then pulled a knife on me, but I got away."

Cassandra suspects she got HIV either from a trick or from shooting up. She ended up in Niantic because of prostituting. She says the cops also tried to pin a murder charge on her because of an incident that began when she picked up a trick and took him back to a friend's apartment. "I tried to shoot him up but I couldn't find his vein, so I just popped his skin. Turns out he's a diabetic and goes into a coma and later dies."

Cassandra's teenage-daughter lives in a detention center and her son is a professional car thief. When he was younger, she recalls, he used to hold her back from johns who came to pick her up at their house. "Then I'd break away from him and hop in the car with the trick and I'd look out the back and see my son chasing after us."

A few feet from where Cassandra sits, Tina, an inmate who left the Marilyn Baker House voluntarily, sorts through a large box of Q-Tips. The good ones will go to homes for the mentally retarded, she says. She wears tight bleached jeans and a ribbed V-neck top. Raised in Bristol, a mid-sized town in central Connecticut, she never knew her father. Her mother was a stripper in a local nightclub and used to store drugs inside her house for the local motorcycle gangs. Tina got involved with the gangs at an early age. To be initiated, she had to sleep with gang members and strip at their parties. That led her to working the streets, because she figured she would at least get paid for having sex.

During one of her stays in Calcutta she picked up "a bad pipe habit." She has been on drugs since she was nine and has multiple learning disabilities as a result, including dyslexia. She spells backward. Tina was one of the first to sign up for the Marilyn Baker House program. She tells us she's glad to be back in Calcutta, though. The drug rehab program had made her suicidal.

"I left because I just couldn't cope with myself, I couldn't understand what they were saying. I thought they were all putting me down." Her pile of good Q-Tips is about a foot high.

"I didn't know what the hell was going on either," Cassandra says.

The women have become friends since leaving the Baker House, although Tina keeps mostly to herself. She tunes out of the conversation and goes back to her sorting, while Cassandra continues talking. "During the AA meetings they'd talk about Bill's story and I couldn't fucking understand it. I was completely lost during the meetings when they'd read the Bible."

A husky, dark-skinned woman strolls by and starts to joke with Cassandra, who tells her I am writing a book about the prison. "I always wanted to write a book about this place, especially about the gay life," she says. Her name is Debbie and she wants to tell her story.

Cassandra leans back in her chair and searches for her cigarettes. "When you come to Calcutta everybody is all ears," she says. "It's like being on the streets. There's no privacy."

Debbie, meanwhile, is revved up and with few pauses, reveals the intimate details of her life. She was raised in various New Haven housing projects, she says. "Now I'm a stud and I've got a rap list as long as your body, so I know what I'm talking about. Now, some studs come in here thinking they're Joe Slick and try to have as many women as possible. They think it's a game. The big difference between black and white lesbians is that a lot of white dykes like dyke women. With black dykes, it's just the opposite. They like femmes. Since I'm a long-time stud here, I'm respected. I put up tents all the time. The COs know what's goin' on inside, but never say anything."

She says she wants to do a movie on this place and how it connects with the criminal life of the streets. For years she has lived like a gypsy, moving from place to place, selling drugs, getting high, coming to jail. She is full of hyped, nonstop talk, her eyes are glassy. Before I can say anything she announces that she has got to split. "We need to talk more sometime," she yells back and disappears through the metal doors leading to the south side.

Cassandra does not blink at Debbie's palaver. It is common Calcutta fare. She is talking with an inmate who tells me she is a Doubleday, of the publishing company. Cassandra gives her a big hug. "We were on the streets together in East Hartford," she says. "We could really tell you some stories."

A couple of weeks later, I visit Cassandra for the last time. I wake her up about 10:30 in the morning. She has been painting window sills and vents in the medical unit all night, until 6:00 A.M. She is miserable. She gets her coffee, pours a half a cup of sugar into it, and we go out into the commons area.

"It's like living in a zoo here," she says. "Everybody's always arguing." The prison psychiatrist put her on a hundred milligrams of thorazine because she has been so tired and depressed. She hates that it is almost Christmas. "I haven't had any drugs yet," she says. "A supply came in last weekend and another is due on Friday. I lay around all day, or work for Colonus and every four hours he gives me a pack of cigarettes."

She complains that nobody helps her in here. "With all the women who have AIDS nobody opens their mouth about it," she says. "The counselors are so overworked they're more like a referral service. They do nothing to help you when you get out of here. The COs drive you back to the streets and as soon as you step off the blue bus it's party time again."

She wants to leave Niantic but cannot until she can show officials that she has a place to go to. A transvestite named Bruce told Cassandra she could live with him. He is dying of AIDS and his house is a shooting gallery. Another woman she knew on the streets named Christine, who also has AIDS, will not give Cassandra her address but writes her and wants her to come home. "They're the only people who want me," Cassandra says. "My old man trick doesn't send me money anymore."

The more she thinks about it, the more she is certain she picked up the virus by shooting up behind Bruce and Christine, all sharing the same needle. The more she thinks about it, maybe there are some spiritual advantages to having AIDS. She has stopped taking AZT and her T-cell count is falling. "I don't want to prolong it anymore," she says. "I'd rather be with God. In fact, I'm coming to look forward to it. The way I see it, AIDS is a way of getting out of here without having to commit suicide. That way God doesn't mind."

A friend of hers named Marlene walks by. She has a smoker's voice and a deep laugh. She and Cassandra start laughing about how everything always goes wrong for them. Marlene's son was killed, her husband beat her, she has cancer, and is about to start radiation. In Calcutta she sells her pain medication for cigarettes. "Marlene always tells me something to make me laugh," Cassandra says. She takes her friend's hand and squeezes it. "With all of her heartache, she just laughs it all off."

After Marlene leaves, Cassandra's mood becomes more buoyant. She talks about how she is going to change her life by staying in Niantic for as long as she can, because at least there is a roof over her head and she is not so tempted to get high.

A week later I return to see how Cassandra is and her friend Marlene tells me she has been released and didn't leave anyone a forwarding address. For weeks afterward, I return and still no one has heard from her. One day I run into Marlene, who is about to start her radiation treatments. When I ask about Cassandra she smiles and shrugs. "When somebody leaves here," she says, "those of us stuck here know that unless they come back, they're most likely out of our life for good. It's a great big black hole out there, and you just learn to accept that."

11

"In Some Ways, This Disease Has Been a Blessing to Me."

When I return to the Baker House, Patty Stoltz asks me about Cassandra and how she's doing. I tell her that when I last saw her, not so good. She twists her mouth back and forth and tenses her eyes. There is concern and compassion in her look, but also fear. She changes the subject. She is no fool. The same thing could happen to her.

Patty and Cassandra go back a few decades. After twenty years without contact, the two women met again at the Baker House. Aged prematurely from the excesses of their pasts, it took them awhile to recognize each other. Once they did, they quickly reestablished their friendship. In one group therapy session, Cassandra told the story of how, when she was in her mid-teens and living at Long Lane, she befriended this young girl from Austria with long brown hair and blue eyes. Patty Stoltz possessed what Cassandra wanted more than anything in the world—a loving mother. Of all the memories Cassandra carried from that period, one of the most vivid was of the elaborate food baskets Patty's mother would send her twice a month. Brimming with German spice cakes, sausages, and rye breads, the baskets were a gesture all the other youngsters longed for.

"You were the lucky one whose mother sent those great big pretty homemade baskets," Cassandra cried out to Patty, who sat across the room. "How I envied you." The recollection touched Patty, but also sent through her a wave of sadness. Her mother had died only a few years earlier, and she had yet to recover fully. In 1960, when she was three years old, her mother took the family of five children from Salzburg to America. Settling along the Connecticut shoreline, she worked hard cleaning houses and doing other jobs to support her children. While in a drug rehabilitation program in Fairfield, Patty received word of her mother's death. That news, among other things, catapulted her into a tailspin of self-destructiveness.

Apart from their Long Lane connection, Cassandra and Patty have something else in common—the AIDS virus. Patty, too, presumes she had picked it up from unclean needles. She is pretty certain she had infected others. The Baker House program gave her time to reflect on those probabilities and to face up to her demons.

Patty also shares Cassandra's frustration with the stigma placed on inmates with the virus. Considering that so many women in the program have the virus, it seems absurd not to deal openly with it. But as someone who has returned to Niantic time and again, Patty knows that the denial concerning the disease runs deep at the Farm and only puts more strain on those infected. Nobody wants to talk about it, as if those infected were the lepers of Niantic. Patty wants that changed. Once settled in the Baker House, she focuses more than ever on finding out everything she can about the virus and how to keep herself healthy. The nurses and counselors at the medical unit load her down with articles and other literature regarding AIDS. She eats fruits and vegetables and takes vitamins and daily doses of AZT. Her T-cell count remains steady.

In early January, she makes prison history when she stands up in front of 150 inmates at a Narcotics Anonymous meeting and announces that she is HIV positive. It is the first time any inmate has publicly addressed the issue of AIDS with such forthrightness. To give her audience an idea of the obstacles she'd have to overcome, Patty tells her life story. The women at the Baker House applaud Patty's courage for speaking out so honestly and publicly. From that point on, Patty becomes the counselor and inspiration for Baker House inmates with the virus. Other inmates whose partners have AIDS also seek her sympathetic ear. Since the meeting is closed to the public, I ask her the next day in an interview at the Marilyn Baker House to recount her story for me. Sitting in one of the small counseling rooms, she takes me from Austria to Niantic.

"I came to Connecticut from Salzburg, when I was three years old," she began. "My mother was a translator during the war and had five children from four different American soldiers. She had been raped when she was younger by her stepfather and her family disowned her. She was raised in orphanages. My mother would make men fall in love with her, then hurt them. Most of the soldiers she was with were married and took care of her until she got pregnant. Then they bolted. My mother also told us that she met Hitler.

"When she was pregnant with me she met a Hungarian. He looked like Rodney Dangerfield. He had been in concentration camps. He used to beat my mother. One time he beat her in the breasts and they became all infected. They were divorced once they came over here. He later pushed his mother down the stairs and killed her. From being in concentration camps I don't think he had any feelings.

"Us Germans are knick-knack freaks and we like everything real cozy. Mother brought us up like in Europe. She rationed all our food, a habit she picked up during the war, and we could only bathe once a week. She made all of our Christmas presents. She also worked a bunch of jobs.

"I started drinking at eight years old and doing heroin at eleven. I sniffed glue, transmission fluid, gasoline, whatever drug anybody gave me, I took. I was a real garbage head. When I was eleven, I started sleeping with this pimp and would go with his girlfriend when she pulled tricks, to rip off their houses.

"I ended up in Long Lane where I was so thorazined out. I ran away from there, moved to Florida, got married, and had my first son at fifteen. A couple years later I divorced my husband and came back to Connecticut and started hanging out with motorcycle gangs, like the Huns, in Bridgeport. I married two Colombians. One, just so he could get his green card and the other one for love. At twenty-five, I stopped taking drugs for three years when I was married to my second Colombian husband, who was a big coke dealer supplying most of Fairfield County. He brought his brother here by paying someone to sneak him through Mexico. His brother didn't smoke, drink, do drugs, or cuss. At the time, though, the New York Colombian mafia was after my husband and when they want revenge they'll kill someone in your family to make you suffer. They shot and killed my newly arrived brother-in-law with a sawed-off shot gun.

"Seven years ago, I was in a drug rehabilitation program and found out that my brother was killed after somebody gave him a hotshot, drugs laced with poison. Then my mother died from cirrhosis of the liver and then her new husband died right after that. It sent me over the edge.

"Since then, I've been in and out of Niantic twenty-nine times—for larceny, prostitution, and possession. In 1989, I found out that I have the virus. For a while I was afraid to talk about it and still practiced risky behavior. I know I've probably given it to other people and I have to try to forgive myself. Now that I'm in the Baker House I'm not ashamed that I have this. You don't have to keep an image here. But you do have to deal with what you were running from. Out there in the general pop they laugh at you if you try to deal with things. Like in the dorms you're just a bunch of animals crammed into a cage. In here, there's more compassion and understanding even though we have our bad days.

"I have an eighty-year-old companion named Poppo, he's the only one who will give me unconditional love. He's stuck by me for the last seven years. I'll probably live with him when I get out. I max out in fifteen months and I'm scared. It's the first time I'm going to have to live legally without hustling.

"But for the time being, I try to learn as much as I can about this disease. I try to keep my mind clear. I'm not afraid of dying from AIDS and I know I probably will because of all the damage I've done to myself. But I try to put all my fears and anxieties to the side because if I don't they're going to stop me from living longer. And that's what I try to tell the other girls. I tell them that they've got to love what life they have left. In some ways, this disease has been a blessing to me. I guess I don't care if I ever find a mate, but at least I know that there will always be someone out there who will love you."

By the beginning of the new year, a few weeks after a third of the original thirty-two inmates have left, a calm seems to burrow into the house and the women who remain settle quietly into their routines. For them, the Baker House becomes more of a home or haven than a drug rehabilitation program. Newcomers often talk about how they want a slice of the peace found by the Baker House pioneers like Patty Stoltz, who carries herself like someone determined to change. She fulfills her housekeeping chores and avoids gossip. If she has a problem that might intensify and result in an assault, she always seeks the advice of COs or counselors, as she had about the foreign language issue. For recreation, she plays Yahtzee, listens to rock music on her Walkman, and reads Tom Clancy adventure novels.

Her appearance improves. She styles her fine chestnut hair, layering it short in front and to her shoulders in back. Except on cooler days, she mostly wears ribbed men's T-shirts with no bra, exposing a heart-shaped tattoo above her left breast. Many days she puts on lipstick and blush.

At one point, counselors bring in a dog from a local shelter to provide a form of therapy for the women. The animal, a mixed breed, has been abused. While several inmates get attached to it, other women complain that it nips at their ankles and frightens them. They want the dog removed. During a lengthy and emotional meeting, Patty helps to resolve the problem. "Look, I'm HIV and I'm afraid the dog will bite me and pass my blood from me to someone else." Everyone grows silent. Patty then adds, "And I don't want to take that risk." The dog is returned to the shelter several days later.

The respect she receives from residents and counselors continue to boost her self-confidence. When a twenty-four-year-old woman named Terry, who also has HIV, enters the program, Patty urges her to go on AZT and think positively. Terry has been a prostitute and sold drugs for some Latin Kings. One day she tells the group how, when she consumed the drugs, as she often did, the Kings would "clear her account," by beating or raping her. There were nights when she was so high she could not get off the floor, and times when she stole donuts because "all my money had to go for that hit."

She continues: "I want that peace that so many of you have found, but I have so many issues." Her father had sexually abused her from the time she was eight until fourteen. Back then she thought it was okay because she wanted his love. "Now I know my street and drug behavior are part of all this. And this year was the first time I really got angry about it. One day I will ask him, 'Why did you destroy all my dreams and visions of a daddy?' Being sexually abused is like seeing someone you love die and then you grieve."

In 1988, Terry had a son and she gave him up for adoption. Until she came to prison this time she lived with her seventy-year-old sugar daddy. "I dogged him so many times," she says. "We never had any intercourse, but I wiped out his savings with my drug habit. He had just retired and was getting ready to move to Florida when we met. He easily spent a hundred grand on me—bought me cars, clothes, anything I wanted. That's why it's hard to go out there and get a job because I know I can't live off tricks anymore."

More than anything else, Terry fears having HIV, because of all the prejudice she has to face. She does not feel it is right for her to have any more children. "I'll never have that penthouse overlooking a river. I'll never become that corporate legend I've always dreamed of being." Terry grows more despondent, her voice fading nearly to a whisper. Finally she takes a deep breath and says, "I did everything I could to get this disease. All my plans for the husband, the kids, the white picket fence are gone. Why did God do this to me?"

Patty sits next to her and listens hard. She always leans back in her chair and folds her arms when others talk. When something stirs her she moves in like a coach priming one of her key players. With Terry's final comment, Patty shoots to the edge of her chair. With little pity in her voice she says, "Just because you're HIV doesn't mean your life has to change. You can adopt a baby who needs it."

"I kind of doubt it," Terry says, her eyes wide and frightened. "I'm a three-time convicted felon."

Patty is poised and ready. "Now just a minute, I found out I had this disease three years ago. Don't ever feel like you asked for this disease, because nobody deserves this disease. To say so is just crazy. We all may have acted irresponsibly, but it's never too late to change. You have to find your own way of accepting it and get on with living. Right now I take AZT five times a day and my T-cell count is going up. I'm trying to make myself strong emotionally, because I think it helps my immune system. You might have headaches if you take AZT for about three months and then they go away. It's a small price to pay to keep yourself healthy."

"Oh my God," Terry says to Patty. "I need your strength. You stood up in front of 150 women and said you had HIV. That took a lot of guts. Help me reach that point."

The meeting ends with many inmates in tears. For the first time, two inmates with HIV make it clear they have nothing to hide. Patty and Terry hug each other, then stand in a circle, joining hands with the other women. A sigh of relief settles over the room, followed by a moment of silence. The Baker House pioneers then raise their clasped hands to the ceiling and sing two rounds of "Auld Lang Syne."

12

The Corona

Another Baker House pioneer, BeBe (pronounced "BehBAY") Vargas, emerges as one of the program's model participants. During group meetings she reveals just enough about herself to encourage other women to speak up. This they all know: BeBe is trying to break out of a destructive relationship; all her life she was always there for everybody, and now realizes her co-dependency is an illness; for once she is doing something for herself by going through the Baker House program, trying to get better and create a productive life.

She takes newcomers like Terry under her wing and warns them: "When you come in here you have to learn to be in control. Because in here the heroes are the people who really apply themselves. It's not like out in the dorms where the heroes are the bad asses." She serves on the welcoming committee, does needlework for friends and for children with AIDS. It is hard to imagine BeBe Vargas ever doing seven bags of dope a day, as she says she once did.

At twenty-six, she has finally found some peace. She looks more like a graduate student than someone sentenced to three years for operating a heroin distribution stronghold out of her Meriden home. She has blue-green eyes, a smooth complexion, and cropped black hair. She has a wholesome plumpness, and her clothes are neat and reserved.

I have heard other things about Bebe from Latin Queens at the Trumbulls, and after observing her at the Baker House for a few

weeks, I approach her one morning in her bunk room. She is working on a needlepoint of red flowers. She looks up at me and smiles. "I
can't talk here," she says and suggests we go into a private counseling room. She motions to another Queen, who is braiding her lover's
hair, to come with us.

"I heard you were in the Trumbulls talking to those Queens over
there," Bebe says, as soon as we sit down. Her arms are folded and
her legs crossed in a relaxed manner. "Did they tell you who the
president was?" Before I can answer she cocks her chin and says,
"I'm the president. Nelson Millet appointed me." I'm surprised at her
candor. She says she knows nothing about Margarita Biblioni, only
that she was a Queen from Waterbury.

BeBe introduces her friend as Maria, her second-in-command or
vice president. She is serving an eight-year sentence for committing
a series of armed robberies with her boyfriend. Though Latin Kings
rarely speak with anyone from the press, BeBe says she is on a
mission to change the image of the "Family" and feels that talking
with me might help to do that. As a "witness," Maria follows the
conversation intently. "When I leave, hopefully within the next few
months," BeBe says, "Maria will take over."

Bebe tells me how proud she is to be a Queen and now a "Corona." To demonstrate her loyalties, she shares the following story
with me: About a year after being imprisoned, BeBe goes on furlough, sniffs a bag of heroin, comes back to Niantic, and gets her
urine pulled. It is positive. Two weeks in segregation, with no visitors, nothing but stone-cold walls, a window to a parking lot, a pot to
pee in, and thoughts, thoughts, thoughts. Thoughts that run through
her like a high-speed train. Or those that stop and hang for hours
digging in real deep, backhoeing to the surface all those monsters she
would like to forget. Two weeks later she emerges from segregation,
from the cell block of her mind, raw, humiliated, shamed. Her two
children visit. They are very young, under ten. They still think they
are visiting their mommy in the hospital. It is the lie a lot of inmates
spin. BeBe prays they never learn the truth. "When will you be
better, mommy?" they ask her. Soon, babies, soon.

She is back in Calcutta. Chaos, no sunlight. As an inmate, BeBe
has served her punishment. But as a Latin Queen she must face
another form of retribution. She approaches two Queens. They're
lying on their bunks smoking cigarettes, feeling each second crawl

by. "I order you to beat me down," she tells them. They look at her like she is crazy. They resist at first, out of respect, but they know as Latin Queens they have no choice. BeBe is a corona, a reina, a princess-queen. Still, she has dissed the Family by abusing drugs. They owe it to the Family to do what she says. BeBe turns and walks out into the recreation yard. The women follow her until she stops, then they block her from the front and back so the COs can't see. For thirty minutes they smack, slap, punch, slug, and kick her—not severely, but enough to make her feel pain. After it is over she thanks them.

From that point on BeBe swears to herself that she will stop taking drugs and seek help. A few months later the Marilyn Baker House opens and gives her that chance. She signs up in late September and withstands all the program's turmoil and growing pains during the first couple of months.

BeBe is friendly but cautious. She paints a sketchy, asymmetric portrait of her life. One big lace curtain. She grew up in Brooklyn, a few doors down from where Jose Ferrer, the singer, lived. By nineteen she had gone to school and completed coursework to qualify as a licensed practical nurse. Then she got pregnant and had a daughter. By then her parents were divorced and had moved to Puerto Rico. BeBe wanted to get out of the city, away from the violence, so she moved to Meriden with her fourteen-year-old brother and her young daughter. They moved in with her grandmother, who loved to party. To support the family, BeBe started selling drugs, and before long supplied a good chunk of the city. Some months into it, she started using her own product, got careless, and the operation crumbled. Before she was busted and sentenced in 1990, she joined the Latin Kings. For a long time, she had wanted nothing to do with the band because in New York, they were responsible for so much of the gang violence. But she had a change of heart in Connecticut, because there it appeared that the Kings wanted to help Hispanic people. As one of the first Queens to live at the Farm, BeBe made prison history.

Maria explains why BeBe makes a good corona. "She is a symbol for the girls. Nelson wanted her as president because she is strong and a good role model." BeBe smiles and looks down at her hands. "I'm just a needle in the haystack of this organization," she says.

Contrary to what the Queens in the Trumbulls had said, BeBe tells me she is against ordering beatings or taking orders from Kings in prison or on the streets. She controls problems and disputes as best as she can through kites and secret meetings at Narcotics Anonymous sessions. Inmates who need money or commissary seek her help. By going through a drug rehabilitation program she hopes to send a message. "My role is to set a good example and to tell the women they must respect the Family's wishes," she says. "Not to start fights or take drugs. I tell them they must prepare themselves while they are here, because when they go home their first obligation is to their children." Her comments sound genuine, yet somewhat stiff and rehearsed.

When I ask her about the Kings' ban on gay relationships, when it is common knowledge that Maria, the Queen sitting next to her, is sexually involved with a woman, BeBe gives her a sidelong glance and says, "It's hard in prison because some women are serving a lot of time and want companionship." She pauses and purses her lips. "But we do condemn bed-hopping." BeBe adds that she herself is not involved with anyone because it could impede her recovery. The Baker House program means more to her than anything, and she does not want to mess that up, although managing more than fifty Queens sometimes makes it tough. "But overall, the girls have been pretty good," she says. "They respect the Family's wishes."

If the "Family" is so good, I ask her, what about its link with drug trafficking and the assassinations of its members who try to leave the organization? She smiles as if to acknowledge the irony, then pauses to collect her thoughts. For the most part, she answers, the Latin Kings are a service organization, out to help Hispanic people. "We have always had to struggle to make good for ourselves because a lot of white people are prejudiced and don't like us. They have no idea what it is like to be poor or to have to grow up sleeping with five kids in one bed. "The police have created this image of the Latin Kings as gangsters and that's a lie," she continues. "There are now at least two factions of the organization and the one we're affiliated with is out to do only good." It is the same clouded story I have heard from every Latin King and Queen I have spoken with, on the streets and in prison.

Later, in a conversation with the program's director, Kathy Mayer, I learn there is a growing anxiety within the group concerning BeBe and the other Queens. Mayer says that if she had had more time to screen the women coming into the program, she would not have accepted any Latin Queens. "The Hispanic women in the program won't speak up during encounter groups because they're afraid," she explains. "One woman said she was afraid that if she talked, the Latin Kings might harm her son in another prison. The Latin Queens simply inhibit the promotion of honest communication."

Mayer is perplexed and asks me what I know about the Latin Kings. I repeat what I've heard on the streets and from police. My take is that although the gang is full of thugs, it has an obscure benevolent element that attracts impressionable people like BeBe and fills them with a sense of altruism and purpose. I suspect that Millet, the leader, talks out of both sides of his mouth. Given the contradictions and inconsistencies of their stories, I am convinced the gang is not as organized or unified as they want everyone to believe.

One morning a few weeks later, I visit the Baker House and BeBe pulls me aside. It is mid-morning. She has on white pajamas, a bathrobe, and thongs. "Last week they wanted to throw me out of the program," she whispers. She calls to Maria, her protégé. The three of us go into the laundry room for privacy. BeBe is on the verge of tears. "The women are threatened by me. I don't know why," she says. "Everybody knows I don't talk to anybody else about what goes on in here. I'm just trying so hard to be a role model for everybody."

Later in the week, Mayer calls the women together to discuss the issue. BeBe says afterward that she came on strong during the meeting and that the women supported her. "I told everybody not to be afraid or intimidated by me," she says, pounding her fist into her hand while leaning against a washing machine inside the laundry room. "That I didn't want my presence as a Latin Queen to hurt the program. That I never talked to anyone else about what went on in the program, and that the only thing that mattered to me was my recovery." She pauses to catch her breath. "They told me that no Latin Queen would be allowed into the program. But now they're just going to highly screen the women and if they are suitable for the program they can come in, regardless if they are Latin Queens."

Of the several residents I speak with, all agree that BeBe should stay in the program. "She's an asset," one woman tells me. "She ain't doing nobody any harm." Kathy Mayer has also come to the same conclusion.

It takes BeBe a while to recover from the confrontation. She tells the Queens throughout the prison not to mention her name or to hold any meetings until things settle. The stress of it all shows. She says, "This whole thing with the Latin Queens has really complicated my life."

Many times when I visit the Baker House, I see BeBe on the pay phone in the hallway between the bunk room and the kitchen. She always watches to see whether anyone is listening. As the weeks go by, she begins to let down her guard and talk to me in a more relaxed, sometimes joking manner. One day I tell her that I want to know as much as possible about the Latin Kings for a story I'm researching for the *New York Times,* and ask if she has a contact outside who will talk with me.

Up until then, most of the stories on the Kings have been told through law enforcement officials. I tell her that there is a philanthropic element in the organization, I would like to explore. She seems very receptive to the offer. "I'll have to clear it through some people," she says. A week later, she gives me the name and number of one of the organization's top officials, Beatrice Codianni. She squeezes my arm and says. "We're really happy that you want to help us change our image."

I have heard Codianni's name before from Warden Dunn. Codianni is notorious among law enforcers as one who orchestrates much of the Kings' activities in Connecticut, and who has subsequently been banned from visiting every prison in the state. In her office a few days later, the warden makes a phone call to see whether Codianni has a prison record, but nothing comes up on the computer. "All I can say is that she's bad news," Dunn says.

At a Howard Johnson's restaurant in New Haven in early March, I stand in the foyer waiting for the infamous Beatrice Codianni. When I spoke to her on the phone to set up the appointment her voice sounded cautious, edged with suspicion. She wanted to know who I had written for, what kind of articles I wrote, and what angles I took. She told me that she had set up a meeting with the city's police chief, Nicholas Pastore, to try to create a more positive relationship between the police and the Kings on the streets, who had complained of harassment. She said she wanted to keep our conversation brief because she was convinced her phone was tapped.

The woman who approaches the foyer at HoJo's looks a lot less imposing than I had anticipated. In her mid-forties, dressed in blue jeans and a stylish black cape, Codianni looks more like an artist than a gangster. As I observe over the next few meetings, black seems to be her favorite color. After settling into a corner booth, we order coffee and blueberry muffins. For the first few minutes she shows a reserve akin to shyness until we start talking about New Haven and the politics of the 1960s and 1970s.

During the next hour and a half, she traces her history in the area where she has always lived. Raised in an Italian family in nearby East Haven, she participated in grass-roots politics for most of her life. She came of age in the late 1960s and worked in the draft resistance and feminist movements. Her political awakening came when the Black Panther party opened a people's free health clinic in New Haven, where she volunteered and helped distribute the party's newspaper.

In the mid-seventies, Codianni became addicted to heroin and entered a methadone maintenance program. "I haven't touched the stuff since," she says stirring sweetener into her second cup of coffee. In 1986 she received three years probation for a marijuana conviction, but has no other police record. For the past five years she has worked as a volunteer for AIDS Project New Haven and for Free Forever Prison, an advocacy group for Connecticut inmates. She supports herself and one of her three sons through public assistance and she does not receive a salary from the Latin Kings.

As reports of the Latin Kings' activities surfaced in the press in the early 1990s, Codianni took note. What she heard and read resembled the earlier days of the Black Panthers, when the Federal Bureau of Investigation discredited them by circulating distorted information to the public. The same pattern, she feels, is occurring with the Latin Kings. "I realize that there was this violent element," she says. "But the Kings also have a lot of positive goals." She has seen how the gang has changed young people like her twenty-one-year-old son Andrew by steering him away from drugs and giving him a strict moral code to live by. She also liked the Family's egalitarian tendencies. "As a feminist the Latin Kings appealed to me. I like the idea that there are a lot of strong independent women in the organization. There are women chapter presidents and regional commanders. You're appointed for your qualities."

In 1991, Codianni began corresponding with Millet, who is serving a forty-five-year federal prison term for armed robbery in California. She suggested to him that the Latin Kings begin a public campaign to change their image, and that they begin by offering AIDS education along with literacy and high school equivalency classes. Millet liked her ideas. "Nelson had gone through a political awakening in prison similar to that of Malcolm X," she says, adding, "He's very thoughtful and articulate and concerned about moving forward." Millet appointed Codianni to the three-person board of directors in Connecticut, making her one of the organization's highest-ranking members. Like a seasoned public relations executive, Codianni will not comment on the organization's involvement in drug trafficking. "I know the only thing drugs will bring us is jail or death," she says. Codianni shakes her head in dismay regarding the execution-style murders of three young men in nearby East Rock Park the previous fall, who according to family members and friends were trying to break from the Latin Kings. "It broke my heart that that happened, but it had nothing to do with the faction of the Kings I'm involved with. People have to understand that there are a lot of violent people out there who claim to be Latin Kings when they're not."

Codianni complains that whenever a street shooting occurs in Connecticut, the Latin Kings are often the first suspects, even when there is no evidence of their involvement. "Contrary to what people think," she says, "members are not beaten if they try to leave the organization. We've had several brothers turn in their colors with no harm done." The press, to a large extent, is responsible for misinforming the public, she says. When she called the local television station trying to get publicity concerning the organization's new direction, she says she was ignored. "The media doesn't want to hear about anything positive. They just want me to tell them where all the dead bodies are."

After the interview, I call two of the agencies where Codianni has volunteered and contact a source in New Haven who has known her for years. Everyone I speak with describes her as a nonviolent and community-minded person who doesn't drink alcohol or do drugs. I phone the federal prison in California where Millet is being held, but a guard tells me Millet does not want to speak with anyone from the press.

Over the next few weeks, I speak with Codianni several times by phone and visit a high school equivalency night class at a Latino-American social service agency in Fair Haven. About twenty Latin

Kings and Queens attend. Many wear the insignia black and yellow beads and greet one another with a special hand gesture and the phrase, "amor de rey," or love of the king. Many have served one or more prison terms. Nearly all have grown up poor, raised by their mothers. Selling drugs is one of the few ways they know to earn money, because jobs are scarce. Some add that people discriminate against them for being Latin Kings.

One boy, Junito, wears his arm in a sling because he has been injured in a drive-by shooting. "They call me Mr. Lucky because I've been shot at fifteen times," he says. "I'm famous because I'm still alive." He calls Nelson Millet his "hero" and says he reads faithfully the Latin Kings' charter. "I was on my way to becoming a gangster but the Family gave me a lot of rules to live by." His breath reeks of alcohol.

Despite Codianni's idealistic ardor, when the photographer for my story returned the next night to take more classroom pictures, none of the Latin Kings showed up. I also made appointments with the young people who Codianni told were good examples of the "new" Latin Kings. Each time no one showed up. I visited one young man's house three days in the early afternoon and was told by his sister each time that he partied all night and slept during the day and refused to be disturbed.

In his office overlooking one of the city's most notorious housing projects, Nicholas Pastore, the New Haven police chief, said a few days later that he welcomed any attempts by Codianni or other members to turn the gang's image around, but that it would not be easy. "There's a lot of leadership qualities in the group," he said. "But society has been intimidated by the Latin Kings for too long. They have to recognize that their reputation is tarnished and there's a lack of credibility."

And Lt. Dan Stebbins, who heads a state office monitoring gang activities, told me that Uzis and AK-47s had recently been seized from the homes of Latin Kings in New Haven and Bridgeport. "These are not the tools to promote a good image," he said.

While I was researching my story, Codianni called me to report that her apartment in New Haven had been raided by federal agents and local police. When she spoke to me, she sounded resigned. The agents took membership lists, letters from prison inmates, and her fifteen-year-old son's baseball card collection; they smashed her video-recorders and some ceramic figurines. She was not charged with violating any laws. "This is like being part of a witch hunt," she said.

Back in Niantic, BeBe continues to extol the virtues of the Latin Kings. She talks about Codianni as if she were a den-mother, and calls her several times a week to report on the Queens in Niantic and to request food or money for inmates.

The morning of the dedication of the Marilyn Baker House is the day BeBe goes before the parole board. While waiting for her outside the hearing room in the administration building, I learn from Warden Dunn that an inmate tried to escape the night before but was caught before she got away. Apparently she climbed up on the roof of a maintenance shed and hid there until a guard found her. Dunn is formally dressed in a navy-blue pin-striped pantsuit and spiked heels. Commissioner Meachum is expected to attend the dedication, and good impressions count. In a culture so often imbued with failure, the Baker House program serves as the pilot for the rest of the prison system and Meachum is pushing for its success.

After Dunn disappears down a hallway, Bob Carini, a counselor at the Baker House, stops briefly to chat. He is a veteran drug counselor and knows all too well the reality of addiction. He is frustrated because so much attention is being focused on the Baker House, yet there is no follow-up program for the women after they graduate. "Unfortunately, a lot of these women are going to succumb to this disease," he says.

BeBe appears moments later, ready for her hearing. She carries a stone in her right hand for good luck. "It's also a worry stone," she says. "Marilyn Baker always carried one. I'm hoping her spirit is with me today." Her hearing is short. After she takes a seat in front of the board, Pascale Magnini folds his hands on the table and stares intensely into her eyes. He recaps her record and then asks her if she has any comments. BeBe sits up in her chair, looking confident.

"I finally admitted to myself that I am an addict and I intend to keep working on my recovery." She rubs the stone in her hand with hard strokes of her thumb. "I realize I have a problem. I hurt a lot of people, especially myself. I had a dirty urine on one furlough. Today I look in the mirror and I like the changes. The program has helped me a lot."

Magnini cuts to the heart of the matter. "How do you resign from the Latin Queens? Stop calling them? Why did you get involved?"

"I felt very alone. I felt like it was a way to help my community."

"You," Magnini says emphatically, "are very naive."

After a short recess. BeBe is called back and Magnini tells her that because of her excellent prison record and her progress in the drug rehabilitation program she has been granted parole, effective in six months. But there are two conditions: she must attend an out-patient addiction rehabilitation program, and she must not associate with organized gangs "like the Latin Kings."

Out in the hall seconds later, BeBe is stunned with joy. She squeezes the stone she had grasped so tightly throughout the hearing, raises it to her lips, and kisses it. "God bless you Marilyn Baker," she whispers.

13

If You're Going to Talk the Talk . . .

"I've opened the doors, I've found all the keys to get at all the pain;
to get at all the shame that bothered me.
And now that I'm here, I don't feel small as a mouse;
I stand tall and proud to be part of a program called Marilyn Baker House."

—Justina

The first graduation ceremony for residents of the Marilyn Baker House takes place at the end of March and resembles that of a small women's college. Held in the prison's chapel decorated with yellow roses and balloons, it begins with a procession down the center aisle lined by family members, friends, and staff. The inmates wear pastel chiffon or cotton dresses, some don gold loop earrings, and a few wrap their hair in French rolls fastened with pearl pins or silk-flowered barrettes.

After the residents sing an inspirational gospel song, Warden Dunn comes to the podium and congratulates the women. "If I could," she tells the graduates, "I'd turn each of the housing units in Niantic into Baker House programs." They all cheer. Two-thirds of the original thirty-two residents have made it through the program, a major feat considering the psychological hurdles many residents have overcome to reach that goal.

Then the warden announces that the Connecticut Alcohol and Drug Abuse Commission has received a $400,000 federal grant to

135

add thirty-two more beds to the Baker House and hire additional counselors. More cheers.

After the awarding of certificates, Justina Jackson, the resident with perhaps the most serious problems to overcome, walks to the altar with her portable piano and sings two songs she has written, both about the Baker House and the painful process of recovery. She looks stunning, like a young Claire Bloom, with her long thick hair pulled back in ringlets. At the program's dedication ceremony a few weeks before, she had mesmerized her audience with her a cappella rendition of "Wind beneath My Wings." At graduation, some COs and staff attend just to hear Justina, the "angel" of the Baker House, sing again.

"When I sing, I love to give people the idea that they're flying," she tells me earlier that morning. "I want them to feel like seagulls coasting against the wind." She opens her song with a long exploratory phrase that gradually lifts like the flight of a bird higher and higher in a pirouetting modality. As always, it is not so much the lyrics as it is the melody and how she controls it and the emotions it touches. She seems oblivious to the power of her voice, and sings as if lost in a trance.

Commissioner Meachum, who I'm told is an asthmatic and jogs four miles a day, sits in the front row periodically inhaling from a white-cupped inhaler. After Justina sings he steps to the podium and congratulates the group, telling them how the Baker House represents a departure from "falling into the trap of thinking about prison as a warehouse." Loud applause and more cheers. The graduation ends with residents singing a soulful gospel song called "We're Gonna Make It," followed by a standing ovation from those in the audience.

The packed reception which follows at the Baker House gives the graduates time to relax and introduce family members. Despite the gaiety, many do not look forward to serving the rest of their time within the general prison population. Those fortunate enough to be assigned a room in Fenwick South will find an atmosphere stable and relatively drug free. Others like Patty Stoltz, who will be going to either Trumbull South or Calcutta, have reason to be nervous. Savoring a piece of graduation cake thick with white frosting and pink roses, she says to me, "It's not going to be a pretty picture."

Ellen Marks will stay on at the Baker House as a mentor until she returns to Massachusetts for a sentencing hearing regarding the multiple robberies, a process that could take six months. Once finished with all the judicial formalities, she will most likely be serving her entire sentence in Niantic. Though she hates being temporarily uprooted, she knows she will be leaving with a new level of contentment and self-respect. "I guess I had to go to prison to finally get my life together," she says.

Justina Jackson has served her time and will return to her family in a suburb of New Haven. Maybe this time, she thinks, she can reunite for good with her two children, ages eight and one. Maybe the spirit of Marilyn Baker will see her through the transition. Maybe, maybe, maybe. "As you can see, I'm an excited wreck over it all," she says, giggling. Her hair has fallen from its tortoise shell barrette. "We shall see, right?"

BeBe Vargas will settle into Calcutta, already familiar territory. For months, she has acted like a Wizard of Oz, dispensing orders and advice from her untouchable corner of the prison. Weeks before graduation she circulated the word that if she heard of any Queen doing drugs she will write the warden and request a urine test. Soon after, however, it becomes apparent that some of the Queens resent being told what to do. At a Narcotics Anonymous meeting, one woman curses BeBe and throws her beads at her. Another woman spits at her.

BeBe remains undaunted and plans to continue her antidrug campaign in Calcutta. Being a "true" Latin Queen gives her strength and will keep her from relapsing. Despite the impression she has left with the parole board, she has no intention of leaving the organization. Instead, she hopes to go one day to Puerto Rico, perhaps under the aegis of "the Family," and develop literacy programs. "Why would I leave the Family?" she says before leaving the Baker House. "This is a life-long commitment."

In the weeks that follow I try to track her down but every time I visit Calcutta she is over at the Baker House working as a mentor. A handful of Baker House graduates now also live in Calcutta. Few have managed to handle the transition. One twenty-five-year-old woman is stuffed with seven others into a cubicle strewn with clothes, shoes, and plastic bags. One afternoon, she tries to write a letter amidst the deafening noise. One of her cubicle mates is asleep, while another sits on her bed with her radio headphones on singing over and over, "I love when you do it to me baby." Down the narrow passageway a woman yells, "You fucking bitches," which is followed by a chorus of laughter.

"It's crazy in here all the time," the young woman says. She has shaved the sides of her head and permed the top into a pile of loose curls. "Everybody in here is fucked up. Every morning there's fights." She gets out of Calcutta a couple of times a week to work as a supervisor of an inmate work crew. Fortunately, she says, she is leaving Niantic in a few weeks. "I'm so sick of all the drugs in here. Kym gets high, Netty gets high," she says, referring to Baker House graduates. "They can't even look at me."

After I leave her, I walk over to the rumbling Trumbulls. I find Patty Stoltz in a second-floor bedroom facing a stretch of woods. Compared to Calcutta, her place looks like a room at a monastic retreat. A mild spring breeze drifts through the window, and the only sounds come from songbirds outside and a small radio playing jazz. Patty is lying on the top bunk, absorbed in a true crime novel, *Deadly Intentions,* about a man who murders his wife. She has on a teal blue T-shirt, which accents her blue eyes, and a pair of faded jeans. "Have a chair," she offers, jumping down from the bunk. She holds out a bowl of red apples and I take one. "People never usually accept food from me," she says with a pinch of sarcasm. "They're afraid they'll get AIDS." That morning she had a blood test and check-up. "Everything's okay," she says, adding that she will probably stop taking AZT, "because it only helps to a point."

Overall, she tells me she is pretty happy. Each week she attends alumnae meetings at the Baker House and workshops on grief and loss, self-esteem, decision-making skills, and preparation for life after prison. Patty hopes to start a buddy system for women with HIV. She pulls up a chair, turns it facing backward, then straddles it. She grabs an apple and takes a big bite. "I was in Calcutta for a week and I was miserable," she says. "But even if I had to stay there I'd be all right. Truth is, this is how I've always wanted to be and I don't want to let go of that."

Patty's roommate, Angie, barges in from the room across the hall where she has been playing Monopoly. Wearing a green cotton prison uniform, she appears to be in her fifties. She looks like a tough cookie, someone who might smoke stogies. The two women have known each other for years, in prison and on the streets. Angie introduces herself as a paper hanger, "meaning I do checks and credit cards." She learned her trade in Niantic and in federal prison along with the craft of "boosting" or shoplifting. "I was so good I could walk out of an appliance store with a television between my legs and nobody would notice," Angie says, then volunteers to explain her daily routine on the outside. I've yet to ask her any questions.

"I'd get up, sniff enough dope to get normal, then go out and swindle. In this last run I swindled about $350,000 in eighteen months." She also received fourteen years for a third-degree larceny conviction.

The conversation turns to the moral codes of street life. Angie rages about how most of the prostitutes she knows with HIV just sleep around, carelessly spreading the infection. She rests on her bed, leaning back on a couple of pillows flailing her arms. Suddenly, she stops short as if she's said the wrong thing. "They're not like her," she says nodding to Patty. "She looks out for the other guy."

"What really gets me," says Patty, who seems anxious to change the subject, "are all these women who keep popping out trick babies. Yeah, dropping trick babies. Then they go out and hustle some more while their babies are alone or in the car asleep. That's why I'm getting my tubes tied as soon as I can." Her mind seems to drift as Angie divulges more dubious adventures from her past: the money she made, the people she swindled, how the high life of federal joints compares with state-run prisons.

I try to steer the talk back to Patty and her plans for the future, but her attention has waned and she has begun to look drawn. On the wall above her dresser hangs a needlepoint of the Harley-Davidson insignia, a gift from a "sister" who graduated from the Baker House. "Only ten of the twenty-one graduates go to alumni meetings," she says. "It's sad because I thought we could maintain our bonds much longer." She knows that her friend who did the needlepoint is in Calcutta and has "picked up" again. As an addict herself, it does not surprise Patty, nor does she express much sympathy. Keeping her own internal moorings in place is about all she can handle.

Like many of the women in Niantic, Patty has no assets and not much family. When she gets out in a few months, she plans to move to a shelter, and then try to find a job and an apartment. "The DOC gives you seventy-five dollars of gate money," she says. "And Niantic gives you five bucks for a cab." She smirks and adds, "Not a whole hell of a lot to start out on."

If that fails, she will go to live with Poppo, her eighty-year-old companion. "What else can I do?" she says with a sigh of resignation. "That's right, folks. One day at a time. You can bet your life on that one."

Back in Calcutta a few days later, a twenty-two-year-old red-haired woman, who graduated from the Baker House less than six weeks before, walks up to me as I stand outside the Bubble waiting for BeBe. She is hyped and tells me she has had a hard time keeping straight. Mostly she gets high sniffing p-dope and smoking marijuana. "I haven't seen any works yet," she says. Her complexion has a yellow pallor and her eyes reflect a deep sadness. On a couch behind her sits a beefy, dark-haired woman with a goatee and mustache who eyes her closely.

"Everyone in here is sick," says the Baker House grad, scanning the cavernous dorm room. "The air quality is unhealthy. They only turn the air conditioner on at night and the filters are filthy." She was raised in a wealthy Connecticut town and got entangled in the suburban drug culture in high school. "I hope when I leave I don't have to come back here," she says. "I hate their rules. I'm tired of having to kiss ass."

Soon after, BeBe walks out of the bathroom with a toothbrush in her hand, all smiles, and we walk back to her cubicle. She has posted a "No Cursing" sign on her wardrobe. Any Queens that do, she tells me, must do a couple of dozen push-ups. A collage of Latin Kings is pasted on her bulletin board. They are brothers from prisons in Chicago, New York, California, and Connecticut. She writes to them to give her support, but not her affections. Nelson Millet gets center stage in her collage, seated in a row of Kings also serving time at the federal prison in Lompoc, California. A handsome man, around thirty-seven, with penetrating black eyes, Millet has the build of a weight-lifter. He sent BeBe other photographs as well, but the warden confiscated them "because" BeBe suspects, "the men looked too tough."

Whatever power BeBe possesses over the Queens in Niantic manifests itself in the small oasis she has created in Calcutta. The atmosphere around her cubicle is like a dome of serenity, no one swears or raises her voice. Inmates, Queens or not, keep their cubicles clean and orderly. The mood is almost cheerful.

She refuses to become caught in the mire of Calcutta, she says. Her life is too full. She works as a mentor at the Baker House each day, attends alumnae meetings, has set up volunteer cleaning committees for Calcutta, and hopes to organize a volleyball team.

"When I first got here," she says, "I'd go into the bathroom and the women would glower at me, but I'd say 'excuse me' and 'thank you' and give them respect. I guess because of my position they thought they couldn't laugh in front of me. Now they know better."

Still, tensions between the Queens and rival gangs divert her from other, more enduring goals. On one occasion, a fight breaks out in Candyland between some Queens and members from the Las Solidos gang, who are serving sentences for stabbing a teenage girl to death. Another time, an inmate named Alicia Gutierrez, who has been suspended from the Queens for using drugs and has formed her own rival faction, calls one Queen a bitch. The Queen, a Baker House graduate, punches Alicia and is sent to segregation after Alicia reports the incident. The episode touches off a fury of assaults, and for weeks the unit is packed with gang members.

BeBe says that Alicia hates her, and often swears at her and gossips about her. One morning BeBe is awakened by a CO who tells her that Alicia's girlfriend does not want to be assigned to BeBe's cubicle because the Queens are threatening her. "But what was really happening," BeBe says, is that Alicia, "wanted her girlfriend with her in her cubicle and blamed it on the Queens." BeBe takes a deep breath. "I always have to bite my tongue when I'm around that girl."

She says factions like Alicia's give the Queens a bad name by stirring up violence and using drugs, the two things BeBe abhors. Not only does it shame "the Family," it reminds her of a self she has worked hard to shed, a self she despises. When she first came to the Farm, she brought in drugs from her furloughs, and sold them to buy commissary provisions for women in need. "I know that wasn't right," she says. "I know that there are better ways. Obviously if we could stop drugs from coming in altogether the staff would have much less work. Everyone would benefit."

When my article on the Latin Kings appears in the *Times* in late April, BeBe manages to get a copy. It appears with a picture of several

New Haven Kings and Queens in a circle around Beatrice Codianni, all of them giving the signature hand gesture. "I know you had to tell all sides of the story," BeBe says to me one day in Calcutta's recreation yard, "but we appreciate you letting us tell our side."

A few weeks later, BeBe goes on furlough and meets several Baker House graduates at a Narcotics Anonymous meeting in Middlebury. The group, all Latin Queens, get a ride to New Haven. There Beatrice Codianni-Robles (she has recently married Francisco Robles, a Latin King) is sponsoring a picnic for the organization in a city park. For weeks after, BeBe talks ecstatically about the event, painting a picture of Codianni-Robles, the Queen Bee, in lively hues.

"She can say things in a way that really brings forth the truth," BeBe says from inside her cubicle one afternoon, with a small crowd of inmates listening in. She's glowing as she adds, "When B. saw me, she picked me up and squeezed me like I was a rag doll."

14

Justina's Return

The news spreads quickly: only six weeks after graduating from the Marilyn Baker House, Justina Jackson is back in Niantic, recovering in the psychiatric unit. BeBe, Patty, and the other graduates who have made headway are stunned. Despite the high probability of relapsing after completing any drug rehabilitation program, no one expected Justina to fall so quickly, if at all.

Inside the psychiatric unit, a collie named Ambrosia wanders the hall while sedated inmates sit in a living room talking or staring at the walls. Justina's room is at the end of the hallway. She pops her head out as I approach and giggles. "Oh no," she says. "I'll bet you want to talk to me." The room is small, painted a cheerful pale blue. It has a steel-frame bed, a chest of drawers, a window overlooking a construction site, and not much else. The portable piano that Justina used to compose her music at the Baker House sits on a chair. A teddy bear is propped on her pillow. "I've already written a song about this place," she says. She has gained about twenty pounds and the blush in her cheeks has faded. She pulls her hair tight into a ponytail and starts to fidget with her fingernails.

When I first interviewed her a few months before at the Baker House, she told me she had been diagnosed with multiple personality disorder. "There's at least three of me," she said, and then elaborated: Justina, "Miss Congeniality," was the artist and entertainer and also the prostitute who strolled the drug-laden sidewalks of Park Street in New Haven. Karen was the fast-talking con artist, hyperactive and in denial about her past. Rin was not as sharply defined. Cool-headed and streetwise, she knew all the cues, and nothing got past her. Sometimes the personalities overlapped. When that happened she blacked out.

She came from a middle-class suburban family, with lots of promise. As a student, she excelled academically and artistically. She acted in plays and sang alto-soprano in church choirs. But by her late teens she had entangled herself in a number of abusive relationships. One boyfriend she dated for years punctured her pancreas, which required emergency abdominal surgery. She later had a child by the same man. When she was eight-months pregnant, the couple got into a fight outside a New Haven bar. Justina said he punched her so hard in the stomach she passed out. Now serving time for assault in an upstate prison, the man continued to send her threatening letters. "I'll show ya what this guy did to me." Justina lifted up her T-shirt and exposed her torso, a horrible crosshatch of scars and skin grafts from her surgery and other lacerations. She looked like someone who had sustained extensive first-degree burns. After her boyfriend attacked her outside the bar, Justina finally pressed charges. "When he gets out he says he's going to kill me."

With the help of her psychiatrist at Niantic, she said she was coming to understand the root of her self-destructive behavior: an amalgam of repressed memories, stemming from the sexual abuse inflicted on her by her father, who died when she was seven. She had no memory of the abuse but was convinced one of her personalities did. I asked her if she could control or bring forth the personalities voluntarily. She answered, "Geez, that's something I do for only my psychiatrist. But I'll try."

Justina sat up against a stark white wall. Apart from a pink hair ribbon, she wore all white. In her Justina mode, she fluttered her eyelids and used quick, dramatic gestures. Then complete stillness. She closed her eyes and bowed her head, taking short, steady breaths. After about a minute, she raised her head. Her body displayed the heaviness of a person in prolonged emotional pain. Hands on her lap, folded as if waiting for something. Eyes half open.

"Karen is fooling herself, you know," she said in a slow-motion monotone. "Justina knows what's going on with Daddy and all that."

The change was phenomenal, but I had no way of knowing whether she was doing it to please me, whether it was real or simply theater, something she performed for her psychiatrist. She carried on, alluding to sexual abuse, then pausing as if waiting for me to ask more questions. Uncomfortable with crossing the line from journalist to psychotherapist, I simply let her talk. She fell asleep shortly after, having said very little. When she awoke, she was Justina once again.

The inmates at the Baker House reacted to Justina's different personalities with nonchalance. "She's Justina today," they would say if I asked for her, or, "Now she's Rin." I learned to match her moods to her personality simply by watching her body language. Overall, her presence gave the house some desperately needed buoyancy, a reprieve from the bog of pain which often permeated the place. She generally didn't get close to the residents. Instead she seemed to float above the action with an ethereal elan, writing songs and poetry, dancing, and singing. She had a gift for turning her own maze of discomposure into art.

After graduation from the Baker House, she went to New Haven instead of her mother's suburban home. There she moved in with an old street friend named Joe, who used to feed and shelter the prostitutes on Park Street in the downtown district in exchange for sex. I knew of Joe from a story I wrote about a street character who lived in the same neighborhood. Joe was Park Street's scam man, he lived on welfare and had initiated a bunch of bogus law suits. He was anything but handsome. Paunchy, unkempt, and toothless, he visited Justina often in Niantic and sent her money. He did not drink or take drugs and told Justina he would help her stay straight.

"Everything was okay for a while," Justina says, sitting in her room in the psychiatric unit. Once a week she would visit her parole officer and go to the Connecticut Mental Health Center for counseling. But after getting accustomed to two-hour sessions with the psychiatrist at Niantic, she found it almost futile to continue at CMHC, where the meetings were short and never with the same counselor.

"My doctor here was helping me to bring all my personalities together, and then all of a sudden it stopped, and I was faced with having to start over with all these different people," she says. She picks up her teddy bear and seats it on her lap. "Anyway, things just started building up inside and I started to get suicidal. My old feelings started coming back. Fear and guilt feelings with nothing to connect them to."

After a few weeks on the outside, Justina began to think of ways to kill herself without anyone knowing it was a suicide. At night she would lie awake imagining herself walking out in front of a bus, staging it to look like an accident.

One day she sat by the window and watched a crowd of people mingling around the street corner selling dope. The television was blasting and Joe had just started to prepare dinner. Justina got up and walked out of the house. Joe called to her in vain. "He knew I was going out to get high, because I went out with this certain walk, the walk I used to do when I went out on the stroll."

Justina spent the next several days binging. "I did P, coke, Valium, I was a real garbage pail." After she sobered up, she called her parole officer and asked that she be sent back to Niantic. By the time of our meeting, she had returned to her long therapy sessions and was receiving extra attention from the unit's primary care nurse. She has avoided talking to any of the graduates from the Baker House, feeling that she has let everybody down.

"I graduated from the Baker House, and everyone was so proud because I did a lot of good there," she says. "Now I'm embarrassed and don't feel like talking to anyone." She starts to cry, then stops.

Justina preens her teddy bear's head and says, "My doctor said that the greatest gift I could give him is to have all of my personalities come together. I want that more than anything else too. God knows I'm sick and tired of coming in and out of here. I look forward to the day when it's all behind me. That's when I'm really going to write some happy songs."

Within the next nine months, Patty Stoltz, BeBe Vargas, and Justina are released from Niantic. BeBe returns briefly on a parole violation. As expected, the Marilyn Baker House continues to grow and grow and grow.

PART
3

"All I ask is, please don't destroy my peace
of mind; it's all I have in this place in this time.
Soon you'll be on your way and I'll be here
still doing time."

—Natasha, an inmate

15

Flowers for the Fenwicks

In April and May, the landscape at the Farm looks
like an impressionist painting. Cascades of wildflowers, forsythia,
and honeysuckle edge the woods and lake, and stands of dogwood
grace the front lawns of the cottages. The vibrant colors, the damp
smell of the earth, and the symphony of songbirds that nest around
Sleepy Hollow draw Delia out of her room and onto the screened-in
porch. Spring is her favorite time of year; with so much nature
around her, it almost makes her forget she is incarcerated.

Spring is also the season of her birthday, a fact she alerts everyone
to months in advance. "I'm a May baby," she reminds her dozens of
daughters and even staff, giving them a wink. "And don't you forget
it." Unlike some people facing their sixtieth birthday, Delia eagerly
anticipates its arrival. When the day finally comes, she gets up early,
says her prayers, and styles her hair in soft curls. With Katie's help,
she puts on a pair of white leggings, a black T-shirt and pink framed
sunglasses. She looks cool and knows it. Katie steps back and gives
her Ma a drawn-out whistle, making Delia break into a deep laugh.
"Look out everybody, here comes Miss D," Katie cooes.

It has been months since Delia has strolled the grounds. Usually
her joints ache and are so swollen she cannot get out to walk. On the
day of her sixtieth birthday, however, she feels like walking forever.
She has missed seeing so many of the inmates from the other cottages, and since she has been too weak most of the winter to go to
church she has been starved for their company. She gathers up her

149

cane and decides that before she does anything, she must visit the construction site for the new prison.

Once outside and walking, the stiffness in her joints pesters her, but she presses on. She ambles past the lakeside where a flock of mallards slice into the still waters, and then up a small hill past Thompson Hall, home of the Segregation Unit. When she first came to Niantic in the 1960s she lived in the dormitory with a handful of other inmates, including Bobbie Moore. Now the place holds four times as many people and has become home to a new breed of inmates she neither understands, nor cares to. Theirs is a world as strange to her as some foreign country. Nevertheless, as she passes by the brick building, an inmate on the segregation side yells from her window, "Hey Miss D, how's it goin'?" Delia simply nods, waves her cane, and walks on. Everyone who comes to the Farm eventually hears about Delia as the inmate who knows the prison better than anyone else and helps ease the pain of imprisonment for so many.

As she comes upon the construction site, Delia can hardly believe her eyes. Covering some thirty-seven acres, the gray concrete expanse looks more menacing than she had imagined. A seventy-five-foot chain-link fence, curved to the inside at the top, ensures no escapes. The structure looks like a men's prison without the watch-tower, stark and imposing. She has heard that the inmates will all wear uniforms and be packed by twos into 8½-by-11 foot cells, each with its own sink and toilet. Once a sprawling cornfield and vegetable patch, planted and harvested by the inmates from the 1920s through most of the '60s, the site later evolved into a beautiful meadow bursting with delectables. It was here that Delia and Bobbie Moore used to forage for turnip, dandelion, and asparagus greens left over from the farming days. Delia can almost taste all those poke salads she used to make to accompany her "blow-out" dinners. Standing some twenty-five years later on the spot, recently stripped by backhoes and dynamite, seems nearly surreal. "They're just going to destroy this place, piece by piece," Delia says in a whisper, "Lord have mercy. Please don't let me be around to see it."

After studying the site for a few minutes, Delia turns around and begins to walk back. As she nears Bride Lake, she greets inmates and COs on foot or traveling in the blue transportation bus. Before long she has attracted a crowd of people, wishing her a good birthday and giving her hugs and kisses. She laughs hard and jokes with her friends, some of whom she has known for a long time, some she has never seen before. Delia, the Pied Piper of Niantic, basks in the attention, savoring every moment.

By the time Delia gets back to her room, she is sweating and breathing hard. Katie fills her blue cup with ice water and she drinks it down slowly. She sits in front of her fan and cools down. She cannot stop thinking about the new prison. "You know they're going to fill that place before it even opens," she says to Katie. "It doesn't matter how big or how many prisons they build, they're going to fill them to the brim."

Since Katie is serving a much longer sentence than Delia, she hopes that officials let her remain at the old prison. Instead of holding every level of prisoner, as it has for decades, the Farm is supposed to become a minimum-security facility, and the lifestyle of the earlier days may possibly return.

At noon, the two women walk over to the lunchroom and Delia comments on how quiet everything is. When she swings open the door, she learns why. Standing against the back wall under a banner which reads "Happy Birthday Miss D," are some forty women of Fenwick South, who break into the birthday song before Delia can catch her breath. The women have decorated the tables with bouquets of flowers they have collected from the prison greenhouse and garden. Dozens of homemade birthday cards dangle from the banner. Delia, overcome with emotion, laughs and cries at the same time. For the first time anyone can remember, she is speechless.

The highlight comes when Katie brings out a chocolate cake lit up with matches posing as candles. The women have each bought a small "Little Debbie" cake from commissary and pieced them together to look like a sheet cake from a bakery. Finally, after lunch is served and everybody has had some cake, Delia stands up and grasps the hands of the inmates around her. "This is the most wonderful birthday anyone could ask for," she says.

Throughout the day, people surprise her. Her "special COs," as she calls them, officers she has known maybe ten, twenty years or more, have smuggled in her favorite foods: Kentucky Fried Chicken, seafood salad, a roast beef grinder, and a strawberry shortcake. Marie Rossignol who lives down the hall, has found a rock-and-roll version of "Happy Birthday" and brings the tape into Delia's room for her to hear. Marie places headphones over Delia's ears, switches on the cassette, and turns up the volume as Delia bobs her head, snaps her fingers, and sings, "Happy, Happy Birthday to me. Yeah!"

By the next morning, the cottage has resumed its normal routine. Though Fenwick South still feels like a quiet suburb inside an urban jungle, slowly but surely the drugs and overcrowding are seeping into its midst. New inmates in the upstairs wing are bringing in drugs, forcing COs to tighten the rules and do more frequent room inspections. Warden Dunn continues to maintain the authorized capacity of the prison by transporting inmates overnight to available state housing facilities. More and more of the women come from Fenwick South.

"I'd rather go myself than see these women pulled out of here," Delia says after comforting several inmates targeted for the overnight transfer. But given her physical condition, it is unlikely that that will happen.

That summer Katie and Lori landscape the front of the cottage by planting rows and clumps of red salvia, snapdragons, and impatiens. To give it some symmetry, they collect dozens of medium-sized rocks, paint them white, and use them to form borders for the flower gardens. Both women work quietly each day, digging, hoeing, and planting like monks lost in prayer. When people walk by to admire their work, they simply smile and return to their task.

The fact that Sleepy Hollow is the most attractive cottage at the Farm makes all its residents proud, but Katie and Lori refuse to take credit for it. Instead they hope their work will send a message to the rowdier inmates coming into the cottage that this is a sanctuary that each resident should respect.

After they finish landscaping the cottage, Katie begins eyeing a shaded patch across the road and decides it would make a perfect spot for a meditation garden, something the residents and staff can appreciate and use. She and Lori circulate the word to COs and the greenhouse supervisor that they need herbs and shade-loving plants. Then she sits down to design the garden. Before long, the plants begin arriving and the small patch is transformed into a beautiful blanket of herbs and perennials. One CO brings in three pine chairs he has built to place at the center of the garden. He has made one of the chairs especially for Delia.

By late July, the women complete the garden and Delia is one of the first to enjoy the creation. At evening time, she takes her water bottle and relaxes in her sturdy white chair, praying or just enjoying the calm. Remarkably, inmates passing by the garden seem to sense its purpose and show respect. Some younger inmates tell Miss Delia that they think Katie is a witch and might place a hex on them if they disturb anything. They refer to the plot as the voodoo garden. Recounting their fears one day, Delia just laughs. "If that's what it takes to keep the garden secure," she says, "then let people believe what they want, "cause I'm not telling them any different."

One day in early August, Katie sits on her bed writing up a list of chores when an inmate pops her head through the door and says urgently, "Miss Delia needs you now." Katie drops her pad on the floor, pushes past the inmate, and tears down the hall. She finds Delia as she had the summer before, propped up on some pillows shaking and in a cold sweat. Katie throws a blanket over her friend and begins rubbing her feet. "Don't worry Ma," Katie says, trying to lighten the mood. "You're just not feeling right because you haven't had sex in so long."

Delia appreciates the joke and chuckles lightly. She grabs hold of Katie's hand and squeezes hard. By then, the room has begun to fill with inmates. One of Delia's "daughters" breaks through the crowd and raises her arms high above the sick woman, and begins to pray. Rolling her eyes back into her head she cries out, "Dear Lord, let the angels come to save this woman!"

Linda Leach, the CO on duty, immediately calls the medics who arrive within minutes, hoist Delia on a stretcher, and take her to the medical unit. After everyone clears out of the room, Katie stays behind to tidy up and pack a bag for her friend: talcum powder, gospel tapes, underwear, crossword puzzles, and Delia's teeth, which are sitting next to her bed in a small cup of water. She walks it over to the medical unit where Delia has been given some Tylenol and aspirin to break her fever and to stop the inflammation caused by cellulitis. Wayne Keck, Delia' counselor, comes by to tuck her in, while Leach makes certain she has clean linens and that her room is tidy. Unlike the summer before when her condition required a ten-day hospital stay, on this occasion, she is back at Sleepy Hollow three days later.

Katie and Lori attribute Delia's sickness to the fear of facing the parole board again, but Delia disagrees. After going through the process once, she knows she will not have to talk about "the accident with Darryl," or her other life tragedies. If anything makes her nervous, it is not having a place to go to if she is paroled. She has already decided she will try to find her own place, perhaps in a low-income complex for senior citizens. The last thing she needs is a bunch of unstable people coming in and out of her life, bringing her down. She will return to New London, mainly because it is small and friendly and has a relatively low crime rate.

After her bout of cellulitis, she stays close to her bed, leaving only to go to church. She asks friends and relatives to write recommendations for her and she talks to Ann Koletsky, who is organizing a resettlement program for women leaving prison. Koletsky has agreed to help her find housing and apply for Social Security and other entitlements. Koletsky has worked in Niantic under the aegis of the Connecticut Prison Association since 1978, helping to match inmates with companions or sponsors and giving them emotional support. She came to the prison at a time when the population was around ninety, and witnessed the drug explosion of the mid-1980s and the subsequent disintegration of prison life. The inmates hold her in such high regard that at the end of the summer, Katie and Lori decide to dedicate their meditation garden to her by calling it "Koletsky Corner."

Delia knows that if anyone can help her get on her feet, Koletsky is the person. During the fall, Delia takes several day furloughs to New London with Koletsky to look at housing units and apply for entitlements. For lunch they stop at the Red Lobster, Delia's favorite restaurant. By mid-fall, Delia's future has begun to take shape.

Still, she approaches the plans for her new life with great ambivalence. Although she will no doubt be happy when her life in prison comes to a close, leaving all of her dear friends almost seems like betrayal. Delia worries about what might happen to Katie and to Bonnie. Both women face years more of incarceration, and the upheaval of losing Delia, certainly the anchor and moral force of the cottage, could devastate them.

Katie always puts on an unshakable front, she has taken care of Delia like a dutiful daughter, and the bond between them runs deep. Losing that connection is a prospect she tries not to dwell on. Bonnie relies on her neighbor for advice about her children and about dealing with the dreary monotony of prison life. She suffers from insomnia and high blood pressure. But always, she can count on Delia to offer some sound advice.

Bonnie's anxiety stemmed in large part from her fixation on the night in March 1986 when her life changed forever. Earlier that evening she drove from her home in Bloomfield, a suburb of Hartford, to have a drink in the city at the Jamaican Progressive League on Albany Avenue. Before the night was over she had shot and killed Joyce Amos, six months pregnant, in a gas station parking lot. The incident and subsequent trial incited a wave of newspaper and television coverage and protests by opponents of abortion rights demanding that Foreshaw be charged with a double homicide. A superior court judge later ruled that an unborn but viable fetus was not a human being under state criminal statutes, therefore she could not be charged with two deaths.

To this day, Bonnie maintains that she shot the gun in the air to scare off Hector Freeman, the man she claims was threatening her, but that the bullet hit Amos. He had verbally assaulted her in a bar across the street all evening, she says, and when she left, he and Amos followed her outside. Continuing to make obscene remarks to her, the man reached into his pocket. Thinking he was going for a gun, Bonnie quickly pulled out a .38 caliber handgun from her brassiere and fired the shot that killed Amos. She says she carried the gun because her ex-husband, who had a history of violence, had threatened her and she needed to protect herself.

Yet witnesses at the scene contradicted her claims. They testified during the week-long trial that Foreshaw had yelled obscenities at Freeman and Amos. Instead of producing the gun from her bra, witnesses said she returned to her car and came back with the gun. The prosecutor, James Thomas, argued that Foreshaw had fabricated her story and that the shooting was premeditated. She was convicted of murder and sentenced to serve forty-five years. The state's supreme court affirmed the lower court's ruling in 1990.

Mary Werblin, the attorney who was working to have the case reopened, told me that the Foreshaw case was a blatant example of gender and class bias in the courts, and that poor people rarely get the kind of representation they deserve. Werblin said that Bonnie's court-appointed lawyer failed to produce medical and criminal records that would have corroborated a diagnosis by an expert witness who testified that Bonnie suffered from post-traumatic stress disorder at the time of the shooting. She noted that he also failed to show that Bonnie had reason to fear Freeman, who had a history of assaults. During the trial Freeman testified that he had argued with

Foreshaw before the shooting and that he had shielded himself from the bullet by ducking behind Amos.

When I contacted Dennis O'Toole, the lawyer who defended Bonnie, he told me that because witnesses testified that Bonnie went to her car after arguing with Freeman and returned with a gun, "that made the post-traumatic stress argument a hard one to sell."

It is difficult to discern whether Bonnie's version of the evening is the truth. Her story, like the other witnesses, is not air tight. But after reading over the court testimony, including Freeman's, I agreed with Werblin that it contained too many holes and inconsistencies to ignore. In addition, Bonnie's medical records, which I obtained from Werblin, clearly show a history of extreme physical abuse. Her first husband beat her with a baseball bat and stabbed her in the throat with an Afro pick. She spent a week in intensive care as a result. The records also show that her second husband beat her and that the police had been called to their home several times. She separated from him in 1986, she told me, but he continued to threaten her, which is why she carried a gun. The records show that she had lost thirty-five pounds and was receiving psychological counseling at the time of the shooting.

I could not argue with Werblin's contention of class bias either. Niantic's economic and racial profile (45 percent African American with a nearly equal percentage of Hispanic and white women) made the arrest and sentencing patterns of the criminal justice system seem suspect. Higher percentages of black women than white women had family members who had been in jail or prison. Whenever I would see an inmate from the suburbs of Fairfield County, I took note because it was so rare. Inmates from Connecticut's inner cities ranked as the majority, as they had from the prison's beginnings.

Because she had little courtroom experience, Werblin set out to raise money for Bonnie's defense and hire a top-gun criminal lawyer. In the spring of 1993, after receiving $10,000 from Marguerite Moore, a Stonington resident and supporter of victims of domestic abuse, Werblin hired John Williams of New Haven. As counsel for the Black Panthers in the early 1970s, Williams had built a reputation as the underdog's lawyer, successfully defending controversial clients. Over the years, he had become somewhat of a local celebrity.

As she waited out the months to meet with her attorney, Bonnie shifted from high hopes to despair. She presumed that the procedure to reopen her case would go quickly, but Williams was in demand, and the wait would be long.

Delia tried to help her through the doubtful times by talking about anything not related to court appeals. The most important thing, she told her, was to try to keep her family intact. Bonnie had grown children, all strong willed, but going through crises of their own. Trying to be an attentive and helpful mother from prison was a challenge.

Bonnie always referred to Delia as her "angel of mercy." They shared a history at Niantic that spanned nearly nine years and each possessed a keen insight into the subtleties of prison culture. Delia hates the thought of never seeing her friend again.

"I'm so worried that Bonnie will fade when I leave" she says, weeks before her parole hearing. "I just want her and all the women here to find some peace." As usual, her black-and-white television with the snowy reception sounds in the background. While she talks, a newscaster tells of the latest drug murder, carjacking, and the details of a twisted child abuse case.

"You'd think the world was coming to an end," Delia says. She could not handle too much news, and preferred to escape into the steaminess of "All My Children."

Earlier that year, Delia attended the funeral of a sixteen-year-old nephew shot and killed in Bridgeport. She later described the scene at a New Haven funeral home in great detail. The boy's mother wore a tight, black miniskirt that showed her red panties if she bent over even slightly. All the boy's friends wore baggy pants which hung down, exposing the middle of their rear ends. During the service the boys approached the casket and stuffed marijuana into the dead boy's coat jacket. At the reception following the funeral she sat and watched everyone get roaring drunk, chasing down whiskey with beer.

"I'll tell you one thing," she says after recapping the event. "When you reach this level of sobriety and see all these people drinking and making fools of themselves, I tell you, it's awful."

Because of "all the craziness" caused by the alcohol abuse in her family, Delia wants to make certain that when she gets out of Niantic, she will find a place of her own.

Many times at night, before she goes to sleep, she lies in bed, fantasizing about what her new home might look like. Bright, clean walls with sunlight pouring in from all over. That is number one. Also, a comfortable bed with lots of pillows, covered with a lavender comforter. A handsome dining room table to entertain guests. Last but not least, an efficient kitchen big enough to cook up her elaborate potato salads and casseroles in advance for family picnics and dinners.

While any number of urgent matters consume her thoughts, her peace is often shattered by a domestic war going on down the hall. Two women who have gotten expelled from the Baker House program for their sexual misconduct have somehow ended up with a room together. They fight much of the time, slamming doors and screaming obscenities. Delia and Bonnie hope the women break up and find new roommates, so the wing might regain a semblance of quiet. Bonnie, especially detests the ruckus. "Here you think you've left all the abusive relationships behind. Then you come to prison only to find all this nonsense being played out across the hall from you."

Delia tries not to get involved, and instead gives her full attention to persuading the parole board to let her out of Niantic. Besides, being the "ear" for the cottage, she knows about more melodramas than she cares to, including the connivances of two women who live above her. Delia calls them the spider women, "because they're always out to seduce and destroy." One of the women got a nurse at the medical unit to fall in love with her. The nurse, who used to bring the inmate grinders and cocaine, got fired. The same inmate had an affair with a maintenance man. Then her roommate, spider woman number two, fell in love with a female CO, who ended up leaving her husband and two children. The CO got fired but still comes to visit the inmate. "These people can be very crafty if you're crazy enough to believe them," she says. "They're real scrounges."

In the late fall, Delia gets word that her parole hearing is scheduled for two days before Christmas. At that point, she decides it is time to draft a letter to the board on her own behalf.

The letter reads in part:

If I am granted parole I know I can make it outside of prison, because I am a different person now than when I first came here. My family and friends are very supportive and proud of me.

I have been working very hard with counselors from addiction services on my low self-esteem and insecurities (that resulted from a tragic childhood!). Most of all we have been focusing on my long history of alcohol, physical and mental abuse. Today I am focusing on my ongoing recovery.

I have used all resources and support here. I attended and completed behavior studies, recovery and co-dependency groups; attended AA and church (as much as my health would allow me). I plan to do the same when I am released.

Delia goes on to explain the details of her transition: who will help her resettle and where. She has been placed on a waiting list for elderly housing and has applied for Social Security and other entitlements.

The letter ends:

I am an old woman in poor health (angina, asthma, arthritis, hypertension, cellulitis). I have thought about my future—I have used my time well here—to change myself and to help others. The officers even bring people to me for help.

I am clean and sober today and plan on staying that way and with the help of my higher power I know I can live a better life, and be a good and productive member to society for the years that I have left.

The board asked me How do you know this?

I know in my heart. I can seek help now. First of all I can go to my God. I never did before maybe that's why I made such a mess of my life.

With the money she had collected from her family while on furlough, Delia buys a black wool dress with a starched white linen collar to wear to the hearing. She plans to wear a matching blazer, white stockings, comfortable slippers, a pearl necklace, and earrings.

The week of the hearing she has a hard time sleeping and wakes up early in the morning, at which time she reads her King James Bible or works crossword puzzles. The morning of the hearing, one of her daughters styles her hair and gives her a manicure. Her hands are shaking the entire time. Katie helps her dress and tries to calm her by making jokes. While waiting for the prison transportation bus to take her to the administration building, inmates and COs stop by to wish her well.

Ann Koletsky, Diane Warley, a sponsor from the volunteer program, and Delia's goddaughter and her boyfriend come to show their support by meeting Delia outside the hearing room. Once again, Delia takes a seat in front of the three-member parole board. Unlike the year before, her posture is relaxed and confident. She smiles and nods hello.

It doesn't take long for the board to come to a decision. The board lauds her for her accomplishments and determination to reform her life. Ten minutes later, Delia Robinson is a free woman—almost; her parole will go into effect that summer. "Lord have mercy," she cries with joy at the decision. "Thank you, thank you, thank you and God bless you all." As she stands up, her excitement causes her to knock her cane across the floor. Carol, her goddaughter, squeals with joy and buries her in kisses. Everyone in the room, even the stenographer, is either laughing or crying. Delia shakes the board members' hands, cupping them tightly in gratitude. The good news spreads quickly through the administration building. Captain Michael Gray, who has known Delia for years, rushes up and hugs her. Other COs and counselors do the same. It is an emotional moment for all those who have made their life's work at Niantic, a bittersweet turning point.

Later that afternoon, Warden Dunn stops by Delia's room to congratulate her. She was just a young woman working as a counselor when Delia first met her. She remembers Dunn as rather shy and unsure of herself. Over the years, she has watched her bloom and toughen, and she thinks that as a warden she is always fair and conscientious.

"What am I going to do without you?" the Warden says, only half-kidding. "Who's going to help me keep everyone in line?"

Bonnie and Katie feel a sadness mixed with joy, and mostly stay away from all the congratulating, trying to keep busy. All day long, inmates from throughout the prison stroll by Delia's window, shouting their praises, like "We're gonna miss you Miss D!"

Delia Robinson embodies a nostalgia for earlier ideals. Long before the 1980s turned everything upside down, and the once bucolic Farm started to evolve into a bona fide prison, there was a certainty that damaged lives could be repaired. Now, no one can say that with full confidence. In many ways, Delia's leaving made the end of an era official. After a decade of rapid change, the halcyon age of the Connecticut State Farm for Women has indeed dwindled to a close.

16

Two Worlds Collide

In early 1994, prison officials open a detoxification unit containing forty-eight beds in the basement of the Fenwick cottages. To the women living above the unit in Fenwick South, the move symbolizes more than just a blow to their privacy. Though the space is urgently needed to alleviate the crunch until the new prison opens, it also shatters the quiet of their Sleepy Hollow like nothing else had before. All winter long and into the summer, Delia, Bonnie, and the other women on their wing hear the women downstairs fighting and screaming well into the night. To sleep through an entire night is next to impossible. The women have access to Fenwick South's recreation yard, and some Sleepy Hollow residents feel they monopolize it. Whereas once the yard held herbs and greens and was used faithfully by one inmate who jogged its periphery daily, it is now crowded with the new inmates, who use it to sunbathe and socialize. Rarely has Delia been exposed to the raw vernacular of the dominant prison culture. No one dares to swear around her, she just will not have it. Now swearing seems to be everywhere. Some of the women Delia describes as "the walking dead," with their anemic skin and emaciated frames. So many she's seen go in and out of Niantic.

They are more like those you'd find in Calcutta, the type criminologists label turnstile recidivists. They straggle in from the streets looking poorly, leave in a few months fattened up and healthy, then return ravaged by street life. As much as Delia dislikes their behavior, she and Bonnie know a few "old-timers" living in the unit, "good-hearted" women who cannot win their battle over addiction, and they feel sorry for them. They make up goody bags with cigarettes and candies, and have them delivered below by a CO. But that eventually backfires. Before long, other women from the center find their way to Delia's and Bonnie's rooms and begin begging for cigarettes and food. Delia and Bonnie try to avoid the women by closing their doors and hiding anything desirable, but that only works to a point. "Bonnie didn't like to be pushed and she'd only take her generosity so far," Delia recalls that spring. "But they know me, and they know they can run me into the ground."

Inmates on Delia's wing often come to her room complaining about their new neighbors and asking her to go to the COs and tell them to quiet down the group and make them stop begging. Delia takes care of the matter a few times, just as she always has for many issues that disrupt the cottage, but she also decides that some of the complaints don't warrant attention. Over and over she tells her daughters and sisters, "Look, I'm not about to let someone jeopardize our space. But at the same time, this is a prison, it's not our home, and I'm not going to get upset at some penny ante stuff like those women down there playin' radios or talkin' too loud."

One day in April, Lt. Diane Sullivan, who has worked in Niantic since the 1970s, comes to Delia's room with some sad news. Myrt, Delia's sister and only remaining sibling, has died after a struggle with cancer. Delia has not expected her to live long, but still, the news comes too quickly. At first Delia feels numb. It isn't until she phones her brother-in-law to get the details of the funeral and wake that it hits her. She returns to her room and spends the day crying in deep, uncontrollable waves, harder than she ever remembers. It is as if the pipeline of pain running through her has burst and she has no way of shutting it off.

Myrt, eleven years older than Delia, had brought Delia to New Haven from North Carolina in the late 1940s. Although she liked to party in the early years, she later became religious, stopped drinking, and lived a straight and steady life her remaining years. She lived near Boston when she died. For most of Delia's life, Myrt was like a mother to her. In the last several years in particular, after Delia had stopped drinking, the two sisters grew closer than ever. Delia often took her furloughs to Boston, staying in Myrt's guest room. At night they used to lie in bed together and Delia would ask her sister about people from their childhood, and they'd laugh about all the characters they'd known in New Haven. When Delia finally got up and went into her room, Myrt often popped her head into the guest room all excited, "I just remembered something else," she'd say, and for another hour or more, they'd continue gossiping and laughing.

There was the story about when the family was still living in Granite Quarry and Myrt had her first child, a boy named Sonny. Delia, who was five at the time, cried for days because she had now been bumped as the baby of the family. It took awhile before she warmed to her nephew, who became more like a brother.

Myrt was more reserved than Delia; although people warmed to her easily, she didn't possess her sister's gregariousness. Out of her seven siblings, Delia alone remains, and it pains her to think about it. Here she is, leaving in only a few months, and she will never be able to spend the time with her sister they had both hoped for. As fortune would have it, Delia has many nieces, nephews, and godchildren who dote on her and are eager for her to leave Niantic. Only months before, at a family reunion, the family had given her a gold-plated plaque which read "World's Greatest Aunt." Myrt's death makes Delia the head of her family, and she accepts the position with pride.

Regardless of her pain, Delia returns after the funeral a few days later, upbeat and grounded as ever. Before she can even rest up, she finds herself consoling an inmate who misses her kids and a CO who is about to undergo surgery. In her mind, helping others is a sure way to dampen her own heartache.

Perhaps the most radical change in the lifestyle of the Farm comes that summer when Warden Dunn declares Niantic a smoke-free prison. Following a national trend that began in California in the late 1980s, Commissioner Meachum decides to make all new facilities smoke-free, and plans eventually to enforce the mandate on short- and medium-term prisons. Concern over the health effects of cigarettes and the potential for lawsuits by nonsmoking inmates fearful of second-hand smoke prompt the ban. Considering that inmates in Connecticut smoke about 75 percent more than the general adult population, the mandate seems guaranteed to create a thriving black market. Throughout the history of prisons, cigarettes have served as prison currency and the core of an underground economy. Even inmates who do not smoke buy cigarettes from commissary so they can barter with other prisoners. Correction officers often give inmates cigarettes as part of an enticement or reward for work.

Dunn plans to phase out the sale of cigarettes and offer classes to help inmates quit smoking. The announcement comes as a shock to most inmates who feel it is a tactic to punish them even further and to create unnecessary problems.

Delia says the ban might stop cigarettes from being openly available, but it will not stop inmates with a bad smoking habit. "You know if they can get all sorts of drugs in here, they sure as the devil can smuggle in cigarettes." It bothers her and the other Fenwick women, many of whom smoke, that the black-marketed cigarettes might cost ten or twenty times the $1.75 per pack they presently pay to commissary, especially since the average daily income of working inmates is only $1.40.

More than anything else, the opening of the detoxification center and the cigarette ban help ease Delia's ambivalence about leaving. She still feels sad that she will have to say goodbye to so many people, but she knows if she stays the changes will only break her down further, and the stress of it all might even kill her.

Too, the chilly political climate in Connecticut is surely casting a frost on Niantic and every other prison in the state. By the spring of 1994, the gubernatorial election campaign is in full swing and inmates—who reckon they have much at stake—follow it closely. Much to their dismay, Lowell P. Weicker, a former U.S. Senator and the state's maverick governor has decided not to run again. Coming into office as an independent in 1990, he introduced an income tax a year later, turning many voters against him. Weicker was also an ardent supporter of Meachum.

John G. Rowland, a former three-term Republican Congressman who lost the contest for governor in 1990, wants Meachum out. After announcing his candidacy in January 1994, he soon becomes the frontrunner by developing a fund-raising strategy that ultimately raises $3.3 million. With an electorate worried about crime and angry over taxes, Rowland's promise to get tough with criminals and repeal the income tax is proving popular.

Using Meachum as a target, Rowland rebukes the commissioner's "Club Fed style" billion-dollar prison-construction program, saying it coddles inmates. Pointing to the $72 million project at Niantic, which includes the new prison and the addition of several new buildings on the old grounds, Rowland says it contains more lavish amenities than the state's high schools. He vows to replace the commissioner with someone whose philosophy mirrors his own.

In April, a few months into the campaign, Rowland becomes embroiled in controversy over an argument he had with his former wife, which provoked her to call the police to her Middlebury home. The *Hartford Courant* fights to obtain the police report, while the police chief (a Rowland supporter) and Rowland himself object to its release. The legal battle over whether the report should be made public continues for weeks, dominating campaign news. A judge later rules that the report should not be released before the election. The dispute appears to hurt Rowland's support among women, yet not enough to keep him from winning a narrow victory that fall.

Delia knows what a Rowland victory will do to Niantic and more than ever cannot wait to leave. By August she has secured an efficiency apartment in a complex of housing for the elderly, located in a safe, well-maintained neighborhood. Friends and family offer to help her out with furniture, and Ann Koletsky and Bonnie Rabelico, a social worker with the resettlement program, help her obtain Social Security and disability benefits.

All summer long, inmates and COs stop by to see Delia, with many saying how things will never be the same without her. Katie and Bonnie try to avoid the topic, but if it does come up, Bonnie stops herself and says, "I don't want to talk about it. I just can't talk about it."

On September 1, 1994, Delia wakes up for the last time in the hard bed she has slept on for years. She has already folded neatly all her belongings and layered them into plastic bags at the foot of her bed. Apart from a wardrobe, a table and chair, the room looks stark and institutional. "I'll never see this room again," Delia thinks with a smile. She's known for a year or more with a bold confidence that she will be okay from here on out, and that she can finally put this stage of her life behind her, but she dreads the goodbyes she will have to face in the next couple of hours.

She gets up, puts on her housecoat, and ambles to the dining room to have her breakfast—oatmeal, eggs, toast, and orange juice. Rarely does she drink coffee but on this day she helps herself to a strong cup with sugar and milk. After that, she takes a warm shower and calls Katie to help her dress. Katie seems unusually quiet but perky. "How does it feel to almost be a free lady?" she asks.

"Well, I feel that the good Lord means for me to go," she tells her daughter in a soft sincere voice. "As sad as I feel about leaving you."

Around 10:30, a CO drives up to Fenwick South in an official DOC car to take Delia to the parking lot where Bonnie Rabelico will meet her and drive her home. Already a crowd of COs, maintenance staff, and inmates from the Fenwicks and other cottages has started to gather outside. As Delia makes her way down the hall and out the foyer, Wayne Keck, who has been her counselor—and she sometimes his—stops her in the hall and gives her a loving hug. Like most everyone who has come to say goodbye, he has tears in his eyes.

"What am I going to do without you?" he says, then turns away.

The next several minutes seem like a dream. Delia hugs and kisses and cries as she makes her way through the crowd, which includes her closest friends, Bonnie, Katie, Lori, and Marie. Younger inmates who claim her as their Ma stand in line, alongside people Delia does not know, but who call her Miss Delia anyway and hug her tightly.

The next thing she knows she is driving through the prison gates and into the parking lot when some COs working in the administration building radio the car and demand that they turn around and come back. Delia cannot believe it. Finally, after another round of goodbyes from the COs and staff at the administration building, Delia is on her way. After she and Rabelico get on Interstate 95 heading for New London, she at last sits back in her seat and breathes a deep sigh.

The highway from Niantic to New London runs past shoebox motels, rest stops, farms, and woodlands. Delia knows it well. Against the fading summer landscape, she watches the cars, trucks, and buses blur by, then closes her eyes and thanks God.

"It's all over. I've paid my dues to that place very well and I'm ready to say goodbye."

Before they go home, Rabelico takes Delia to pick up some groceries. Her sponsor from Niantic, Diane Warley, is already there washing windows and making things cozy. Delia's goddaughter Carol and her daughter also plan to help her settle in. Her old friend Martha Garvin, a former CO and spiritual mentor of Delia's, is also expected.

The next thing Delia thinks about is dinner. Maybe some steamed greens, pork chops, and some iced tea to wash it all down. She will celebrate and welcome any guests by making one of her famous cakes, the one with the thick icing topped with colored sprinkles. So, so many things to look forward to. Delia makes a list in her head of all the things she wants to accomplish over the next few days and weeks. Her days now belong solely to her. By the time they arrive at her new home, Delia Robinson, former resident of the Farm in Niantic, feels like a self-assured cloud in a boundless sky.

17

Another Chance

The group home at the end of a winding road over-looks the Connecticut River. On the second floor in a room with windows offering three different views, Delia fusses over two elderly residents named Mary and Joey, both of whom are mentally retarded.

Mary paws and tugs at Delia's sequined T-shirt with the designs printed around the border. "Those are pineapples. Those are pineapples," Mary insists. Delia chuckles. "Oh, I see. I didn't know that, Mary."

Mary, in her early eighties, whispers to Delia about her imaginary friends, like the woman who walks around the home wearing only a bra and tennis shoes, and the old man who lives outside in a junked car and shouts dirty words to her.

"You know what we're gonna do, Mary? We're gonna find that man and wash his mouth out with soap," Delia tells her as she brushes back the hair from the old woman's face.

Mary blushes and nods her head. "Yeah, we're gonna wash his mouth out with soap." She turns to the television and starts talking to it.

Meanwhile, Delia helps straighten Joey, who is slumped over in his wheelchair. He has spent most of his fifty-some years in a wheelchair, and has repeated over and over for much of that time, "I'm stuck! I'm stuck!"

When he wants Delia's attention he tucks his hands into the V-neck of his shirt and continues shouting, "I'm stuck!"

"I have those days too," Delia says looking him straight in the eye. Joey rolls his eyes back and starts laughing. "I'm stuck!"

Pulling each hand out of Joey's shirt, Delia places them lightly on his lap, then rubs his shoulder affectionately.

Mary sits and talks to herself using dainty hand movements. She is embarrassed if her slip shows and constantly checks it. She grabs Delia's hand and calls her "the nice colored lady." Delia chuckles again. Then Mary points to Joey and says, "He's a crazy man."

Four days a week, for a total of twenty hours, Delia comes here or to another group home to work as a companion for several elderly mentally retarded residents. She got the job by answering an ad in the newspaper. After the supervisor of the agency met her and called a few references she hired Delia immediately. She gets paid a small stipend for her work, which does not conflict with the Social Security and disability payments she receives of $460 dollars a month. She loves the work and the challenge of caring for Mary and Joey. She has been out of Niantic for over a year, though to her it seems like ages.

After Delia was released, Diane Warley and Ann Koletsky threw a surprise shower for her at her goddaughter's home. For Delia, who left the Farm with nothing but her clothes and a few personal items, the party was the crown jewel in her new life. It took two cars to carry to her apartment the gifts she received: kitchenware, linens, and most loved, a lavender bedspread. Before long, her small home radiated coziness and cheer. It is filled with crocheted pillows and lace curtains, and has bright walls, plenty of sunlight, and a kitchen big enough to cook her famous home-style meals.

Gradually Delia began to explore her neighborhood. She and her goddaughter Carol started attending the new Baptist church down the street, and Delia found a country grocery store which sold southern foods like collard and mustard greens, okra, and chitlins. She made a few good friends in her complex who stop often for coffee and cake.

Though most of her relatives live in New Haven, some fifty miles away, they have been a vital part of her new life. Her nieces and nephews call or visit her regularly and Sonny, Myrt's son, drives from New Haven a few times a month. Once Delia invited a former CO from Niantic to come to New Haven to meet her family. The woman said to her afterward, "Delia, I've never seen a family love someone like yours loves you."

This love was evident at a welcome-home barbecue attended by some seventy-five relatives and friends following Delia's release. One of the day's highlights came just before Delia's oldest friend Libby served ice cream and cake. A crowd of well-wishers gathered in the living room to hear Delia's nephew Jerry serenade his "Aunt D" with a love song. A professional singer with a haunting tremolo, he performed the piece holding his hand to his heart. Later one of Delia's nieces said to me, "We all suffered with her through the tragedy. Now we just want to take care of her like she always took care of us."

Despite the support of family and friends, Delia's transition from prison to civilian life has had its bleaker moments. After the shower, the settling in, and the barbecue, the realities of day-to-day life soon set in. In Niantic, Delia was always surrounded by people. Now, with most of her friends and family living miles away, she often found herself alone for hours and sometimes days. Out of prison only a couple of months, she began to feel the onset of a depression. In the late fall she found a babysitting job for four days a week, but that fell through a few weeks later when she found out that the young, single mother was unreliable and a drug addict. Although she had gotten close to the woman's two young children, she said it was better for her health to stay out of that situation. "I've been around enough of those people," she said. "At this point in my life, I need stability from everyone around me."

Delia's depression was compounded when a friend's daughter stole an envelope Delia had hidden inside her Bible containing money to pay her rent and bills. When Delia's niece heard about the misfortune, she sent the money to her aunt the next day by Federal Express. Still, Delia had done so much for the young woman who stole the money that the act seemed like a betrayal and downright irony. No one had ever stolen from her in Sleepy Hollow.

Knowing how dangerous her depression could be, Delia scanned the newspaper daily looking for something to fill her time. She had worked most her life, and despite her health problems she hoped to continue, even on a volunteer basis. "You know I just can't sit around here all day," she would say. "I've got to be doing something useful."

Through it all, however, she felt blessed to be on the outside. When the new prison opened in October 1994, Delia read about it in the New London newspaper, while relaxing in an easy chair inside her apartment. It was named the Janet S. York Correctional Institution in Niantic, after the former warden, who also gave the keynote address at the dedication. As Delia and others had predicted, the state was already making plans to expand the 550-bed facility by building two more housing unit, containing 196 beds each. Delia remembered that the original plan called for only 350 beds. She also recalled that when she began her last sentence in 1985, the population was around three hundred, now it was edging closer to twelve hundred inmates.

Connecticut's new governor, John Rowland, who had criticized the new prison as too elaborate, was getting ready to appoint someone to replace Commissioner Meachum, who had accepted a position with the U.S. Department of Justice. At the dedication, Meachum responded to Rowland's charges by saying, "In today's climate of hate-rhetoric, this facility is atypical, but it will be here when philosophies evolve and come back."

Delia recalled reading the article as though it were a great drama she had the privilege of watching from the sidelines. She kept in touch with Bonnie and the other women from her unit, by letter and occasional phone calls. A few months after Delia's release, the Marilyn Baker program was moved to Fenwick cottage, her former residence. The north side is used for residents and the south for alumnae, with a total of about eighty-five inmates. Bonnie, Katie, and the other women in the unit were uprooted and moved to the rumbling Trumbulls. Delia learned that the move proved particularly hard for Katie, because Lori had been released from prison and moved south.

Right before Christmas, Delia picked up her morning paper and read that Beatrice Codianni-Robles and thirty-two other Latin Kings were indicted on racketeering charges by a federal grand jury. The indictments alleged that Codianni-Robles and five other gang members plotted to kill a rival in March 1993, the same month I had spent interviewing her. Law enforcement officials charged the Kings with killing or wounding people who threatened the gang or its dominance of the crack, cocaine, and heroin trade in New Haven and

Bridgeport from 1991 to 1994. Codianni-Robles was not charged with any of the murders. The list of Queens indicted did not include BeBe Vargas, whom Delia had known of in Niantic.

The most stunning news Delia received came in the spring of 1995 through a phone call from a prison staffer. Though the details the staffer gave her were sketchy, Delia learned that Carol Dunn had retired unexpectedly and was replaced by the Farm's first male warden. The swift and puzzling turn of events saddened many staff and made them fear for their jobs. Dunn's departure signaled that the wrath of the Rowland administration had finally taken hold. Letters Delia received from inmates now compared Niantic to a boot camp.

After Delia started her job at the group home, her depression subsided. Her enthusiasm was apparent in all the stories she told about the people she took care of and how they had changed her own thinking about the mentally retarded. She was meeting new people too, but tried to keep those relationships on the professional level.

Except for her family and friends, few knew about her past, and Delia worked at concealing the hard facts. With new friends she kept the conversation about her past vague and to a minimum. Always friendly and polite, she seldom went down to the common's lounge and stayed mostly in her apartment. She was often visited by relatives and friends, who rarely left without a cake or casserole in their hands.

Once at work, a young supervisor asked whether she had any children. Delia told him she had a son, but that he had died. The supervisor must have sensed her reluctance because he immediately changed the subject. "Nobody's going to ask a mother who's lost her only child a bunch of questions," she told me. It was the spring of 1995, a few months after she had started her job. We were driving around New London running errands and enjoying the spring weather. On the way to pick up her dinner at Kentucky Fried Chicken, Delia asked me to turn into a residential section of two- and three-family homes. After a few blocks, she pointed down a steep side street. "That's where Darryl and I used to live, and that's where the accident happened," she said. She said nothing more, and I decided not to drive down the street, but for the next several minutes Delia remained unusually subdued.

Over the two and a half years I spent interviewing Delia, she rarely talked about her son, yet when she did it was apparent that he was never far from her mind. On the same day we drove past her old street, we also talked about how the choices one makes in life shape character and destiny. "I had a lifetime of making bad choices," she said. "And it wasn't until I went to prison that I finally learned how to make good choices. If it weren't for all those people in Niantic, I probably wouldn't be here."

At the group home, she jokes with Mary and Joey and they respond with smiles. After a few minutes, she wheels Joey outside to get some fresh air. Under a dogwood tree, Joey raises his eyes to the sky and beams every time he hears Delia laugh. "I wish I was an expert in the way their minds work," Delia says. "There's nothing predictable about Mary and Joey. They're always full of surprises."

She sits back on the shaded bench and inhales her cigarette, then stubs it out. Breathing hard, she releases the brakes on Joey's wheelchair and wheels him back inside. She doesn't want to be away from Mary too long, she says. Mary rarely goes outside and is waiting for Delia in a chair near the nurses' station. The three join up and decide to go back into the sunroom, Delia pushing Joey's wheelchair, Mary following swiftly in her walker. "I'm stuck! I'm stuck!" Joey repeats over and over. "I know that feeling," Delia says with her infectious belly laugh.

When one of the Baker House pioneers had written two years earlier, "there is no gain without pain; that to endure life we must struggle to meet challenges and stand tall and proud in the face of our own worst enemy," she could have been speaking about any woman in Niantic trying desperately to remake her life, but she certainly spoke for Delia Robinson. Out of the dozens of women I interviewed, she was one of the few who rarely made excuses for why she was in prison. Determined to shed old habits and face down painful memories, she now looked forward to a full and stable life.

"For the first time in years I'm a happy lady," she tells me a few days later, sitting in her living room. Despite her busy schedule, her home is as tidy as her room was in Niantic. A stunning picture of her mother, Cardie, hangs in her foyer. She still keeps her television on most of the time while she works on her crossword puzzles. The hallway to her apartment is usually redolent with the smell of pork and beans, pineapple upside-down cake, or sweet potato pie. Never far from her easy chair sits her plastic blue cup, the one Katie and

Lori used to fill every morning with ice water. She misses her friends, she says, and hopes that when they do leave Niantic they have as much support as she has had over the past year. God willing, she will be there for them, as always. "May the good Lord help us all," Delia says.

She sits back in her chair and starts talking about her job, letting out a good-natured laugh over something Mary has said to her. She wants to find out all she can about Mary and Joey and their disabilities. The nurses at the home have told her how much the two residents have improved since she arrived. "They're like my kids," Delia tells me. "All I want to do is make them happy."

Epilogue

Carol Dunn has moved on with her life and is now working as a supervisor at the Hartford Juvenile Detention Center. I visited her at work in late 1995, several months after she left Niantic. Instead of the tailored business suit I'd been accustomed to seeing her in, Dunn greeted me wearing a casual tunic and slacks. Apart from a new hair style, she had not changed. She told me it was her forty-third birthday.

The detention center was undergoing a major renovation both physically and philosophically, and Dunn was one of the correction professionals brought in to reshape its direction and upgrade its programs. She was obviously more than qualified. Before we settled down to talk, Dunn showed me around and introduced me to her colleagues. She talked about her new job with the same exuberance that she had had three years earlier as the new warden for Niantic. "In a sense it's Niantic all over again," she said. "Only this is where it all starts."

After showing me the new construction plans for the center, we settled into a staff lounge and she began talking about her days at the Farm, the notorious inmates she had known, and some of the staff she had been friends with since her early twenties. "One day I want to write about my experiences, too," she said.

Without the constraints of her former title, Dunn seemed relaxed and much more candid. "I really didn't want to leave when I did," she said. Indeed, she had looked forward to finally getting the overcrowding problem solved and focusing her attention on programs for inmates. But soon after being appointed, the new DOC commissioner John Armstrong shook down the correctional system by relocating more than half of the twenty-eight wardens throughout the state to different prisons. Dunn was told she was being transferred to the Carl Robinson Correctional Institution, a medium-security prison seventy-five miles from her house. After she said the commute was out of the question, she was offered her former post at the Brooklyn Correctional Center, for a $12,000 cut in pay. "I was so stunned," she said. "I kept on thinking, my God, why are they taking my dream from me?"

Since she could not afford the cut in pay, she realized she had little choice but to retire. Many of the staff expressed their sadness and shock. At times she had to close the door to collect her emotions. The weeks before her departure were hell.

"I don't want people to think I'm bitter, but things should have been handled much differently," she said. Her eyes were teary and sad. She took a deep breath as if to push it all away. "Though I'm fortunate because one door closed and another one opened for me. I'm confident that others at the prison will carry out what I hoped to do."

I returned to Niantic that same month, after not seeing the place for about a year. Dunn's legacy was firmly intact. Preliminary studies had shown a significant drop in the recidivism rates of women who had completed the Baker House drug program. After tracking inmates for a year after their release, researchers found that only 23 percent of those who had graduated from the Baker House program returned to custody, compared with 77 percent of inmates who did not have any substance abuse treatment. The Baker House now had a strong alumnae and mentor program and tighter screening procedures for applicants.

The entire prison looked scrubbed down and less crowded (with the new prison next door, the population had dropped by about 100 inmates). The cottages and Davis Hall had received a fresh coat of paint. The ban on smoking had vastly improved the air quality, though I had heard that black-marketed cigarettes were now going for about forty dollars a pack. Before Dunn left, she had a screened-in gazebo built on the grounds for staff who smoked. A wellness center for staff now operated out of an old brick house near the entrance. There were also new administrative offices, a stunning new gymnasium, and a glassed-in cafeteria.

Calcutta had also undergone a transformation for the better. The walls were now a soft lavender, and acoustic panels hung from the ceiling to absorb the noise. Gone was the congestion and chaos of a couple years back. Overall, the old prison seemed more at peace. Officials had disbanded the Segregation Unit in Thompson Hall and started converting the building into a parenting program. Gang activity and drug trafficking, Warden Ed Davies told me, were almost nil. "If we have any problems we send them next door. My biggest contraband issue is the cigarettes."

Niantic by the end of 1995 had become what Dunn, Elizabeth Gilchrist, and other staff had hoped it might, a stabler atmosphere with fewer inmates and disciplinary problems. I couldn't get a feel for the overall mood of the institution; it seemed more formal perhaps because I was with the new warden the whole time, which undoubtedly colored things. I had come just to see the physical changes, not to interview inmates. I didn't need to.

From my correspondence with staff and inmates I knew that the Rowland administration's "get tough" philosophy now dominated the atmosphere, at least in theory. Davies himself gave me that impression with his reluctance to talk about programs and his emphasis on "inmate accountability" and "public safety." Nevertheless, treatment and behavioral programs seemed secure.

During our tour, I recognized several inmates who had left and returned, including an acquaintance of Cassandra's who told me she had loss track of her, and an inmate who had graduated from the Marilyn Baker House. I also ran into some of the long-termers, like Bonnie and Katie, who now taught music classes for inmates. Bonnie was still waiting for a hearing to reopen her case. "Everyone seems so positive," she told me. "It's so hard to contain what I feel. Freedom is so close I can taste it, yet so far away because I don't know what the judge's decision will be." I sensed that she and Katie didn't feel comfortable talking to me with the warden around, so I kept the conversation brief.

Davies had been transferred from Carl Robinson, the prison where the DOC wanted to send Dunn. In 1994, an inmate riot there resulted in the deaths of two prisoners. In his new office at Niantic, he recalled the conflagration. The effects of the ordeal became apparent in his voice and body language. "It'd been a difficult year," he told me. "So Niantic was a nice change."

Later as we passed a group of inmates raking the fruit orchard, first planted the summer I began my research, Davies told me he wanted to plant a garden in the plot next to it, to help structure inmates' lives. The food would go to homeless shelters and soup kitchens. I didn't want to say it, but it sounded like deja vu.

Davies was still in the honeymoon stage with the staff, who gave him credit for supporting many of the old programs and trying to create an atmosphere of respect. Others doubted his commitment to Niantic and predicted he'd move on to a more opportune position within a year. Unfortunately, he cut our interview short, saying he'd received a call from his boss and had to take care of another matter. Knowing what was "goin' down" that week behind the scenes, I realized my visit was badly timed. An inmate had accused the prison's deputy warden, Robert Shukas, of sexual assault. About the time of my visit, Shukas had been pulled off grounds to work at the DOC's headquarters while the department launched an internal investigation. Given Shukas's ranking, the staff viewed it as an act of betrayal and one more blot on the escutcheon of Niantic. I had heard rumors from inmates for several months about Shukas's involvement with a Latin Queen. Curiously, during the time I conducted the bulk of my research, Shukas was in charge of monitoring gang activities.

Shukas was arrested and formally charged with sexual assault within weeks and the local press had a field day. Television stations flashed shots of cheap highway motels where the couple's rendezvous allegedly took place while the inmate was on furlough, and newspaper accounts detailed the inmate's description of an identifying mole on Shukas's lower abdomen.

After meeting with Davies, I ran into Teresa Lantz, the warden of the Janet S. York Correctional Institution, the new maximum-security prison next door, who agreed to give me a tour of the facility. The following week, as I drove into the parking lot of the compound, I was surprised how much it resembled a community college. The buildings, low and modern, displayed an academic motif with contemporary angles, honeycombed walkways, and a circular drive. After being searched by a correction officer, I made my way through two locked steel doors on the way to Lantz's office. We met in a conference room where the lights were controlled by movement. She offered me coffee and her homemade apple pie.

Despite the cozy tone, Lantz made it clear that she was a political animal, faithful to the new administration's credo of ensuring public safety and inmate accountability. She told me I wouldn't be able to photograph anyone inside the prison and could only interview an inmate if I had a "good reason," and that interviews would be monitored. When I described how I had spent nearly eighteen months in Niantic interviewing inmates with little supervision, she told me, "There's no way you'd be able to do that today."

Limiting media access to inmates was another growing trend in corrections. The new policies are meant to protect victims' rights, after complaints that media coverage glorified criminals, ignored victims, and caused great pain to their families. There have been plenty of stories of that nature, mostly promulgated by the unfortunate tabloid news mentality of recent years. Yet by narrowing access, the policies assume that prison conditions always meet the legal standards for health and safety, that inmates have no legitimate grievances, and that the court system is infallible, sending to prison only those who are guilty. While I hear a lot about inmate accountability, the new policies do not bode well for prison accountability.

After we had talked a few minutes, Lantz asked me what my schedule was like. I told her I was flexible. "I'll give you the rest of day," she said. And she did. The tour of the prison started at an expansive entryway, a corridor with skylights, glass, and immaculate tiled floors. Although it looks extravagant for a prison, Lantz told me, the design called for the use of cheaper materials like split concrete to give the walls a quartzlike appearance. Still, it far surpassed what I had expected. Lantz showed me modern classrooms and a new data-processing center for inmate training and employment. Beyond, on the prison grounds, inmates walked by in blue and burgundy uniforms speaking in quiet tones as COs stood on the sidewalk monitoring their activities. Near the restrictive housing building stood exact replicas of the gymnasium and cafeteria next door. Surrounded by a well-landscaped lawn, the symmetrically aligned rows of housing units resembled college dormitories. Construction had begun on another one to house 196 more inmates. In the far distance lay a baseball field.

Despite the stunning architectural display, the atmosphere seemed Orwellian. The COs I met in one housing unit were fresh out of the training academy, polite but stone-faced. Inmates were locked by pairs in spartan cells, with toilets, sinks, and windows with a view to the courtyard. Their movements were electronically monitored. The stark physical details and confinement rules are necessary to maintain order, Lantz told me. "The system is set up to reinforce structure. You are locked up unless you're going to work, to school, or to a program. This automatically instills discipline, which helps to build self-worth and maintain control of the population."

Lantz unlocked one of the prison cells with two women inside. One of the women looked at me and asked, "Are you the warden?" Lantz immediately spoke up and introduced herself. As a male guard for the unit stood by, the inmate told her, "That man talks to us with no respect. He calls us animals and says because we're in prison we deserve to be locked up." By her look, it was not something Lantz had anticipated. She told the guard she would speak to him later. As we walked on, she said that when COs transferred from male to female prisons, they often needed to change their approach. "I often have to tell staff coming to work here for the first time that here we don't call the women 'girls' and we don't talk to them like children."

Before I left, Lantz said researchers from the National Council on Crime and Delinquency had interviewed inmates at York for a study on women in prison. Leslie Acoca, a senior researcher for the council had spent three years examining women's maximum-security prisons nationwide, one of which was the new one in Connecticut. She told me that York's medical facility, its architecture and overall management approach, which encouraged inmates to use their time constructively, made it one of the best in the country. Citing the institution's design as a key feature she said, "One of the hopeful aspects of Connecticut's prison is that it's definitely built for women, not men. It was the only prison where I didn't feel physically depressed."

When I tried to get the staff's reaction to Acoca's observations, no one would speak to me on the record. The decades-old philosophy of the Farm remained deeply embedded in the hearts of many, who viewed the new confinement rules as dangerous. One staffer, who had worked for years at the old prison and now worked at York, said that if the new prison was one of the best operating women's prisons in the country, then "that's really pathetic." The staffer added, "So many women had come to Niantic and it was safe and it was home. We made it a positive experience. The whole confinement model concept is so short-sighted. These people are going to be less equipped and more angry. In the long run it's not better for the public's safety."

Another long-time CO compared York to the old Brooklyn zoo, "where the animals are locked in cages and the guards become afraid of them and the animals finally strike back."

Newer COs at York felt the old philosophy at Niantic infantilized women, a complaint that had circulated for years. At the same time they said that the new compound was too extravagant for prisoners and that the money should have gone to build schools. Their stance toward inmates was far less sympathetic than those who had been connected to the prison for a longer stretch.

The two compounds in Niantic represented a clash in cultures between the tough management policies of the mid-1990s and the old but defiant rehabilitation model. From my own observations inside a women's prison, I could not agree with confining such large numbers of inmates in locked cells. I knew from dozens of studies that the vast majority of women in prison are not violent, and confining those that are not is counterproductive. The system is avoiding the real issues that bring most people to prison in the first place. But, as Acoca pointed out, what made York different from similar systems was the potential of strong behavioral, substance abuse, and education programs as an incentive for getting women out of their cells and idleness. Good behavior might even result in moving to the original prison where life was much less harsh. Though I felt the system was far from perfect, by separating inmates by the degree and severity of their crimes many more inmates benefited, particularly those living in the cottages on the original grounds.

Elizabeth Gilchrist, who had been promoted to acting captain at the old prison in early 1996, called the changes a relief because they enabled Niantic to regain some of the dignity it had lost over the past decade. To her, the Farm was like an old friend who had been ill for years and had finally been restored to some modicum of health. One of her new tasks included assembling the first archive for Niantic. After nearly thirty years of working at Niantic and serving under a succession of wardens, Gilchrist now threw her heart into piecing together and safeguarding the history of the Farm. Like a loyal veteran, she insisted that the prison's future held plenty of promise. "If I didn't believe that things would eventually work themselves out, I would have left by now," she said to me. "Yet I still love this place, because I know there's hope."

Still, as she had once pointed out, Niantic was not meant to be a cure all. Gilchrist knew as well as anyone that all the programs and new philosophies would not necessarily keep people from coming back again and again. The return rate of inmates to Niantic had run about 70 percent for some time. Among the inmates I interviewed, it was not so much the fear of being in prison that concerned them, but rather the fear of getting out. My sense was that the $72 million the state had poured into the prison was poorly spent. Though a good portion of the funding was needed to build new housing for the growing population and upgrade facilities, one study after another has shown that incarceration is neither the most viable or cost-effective punishment for the bulk of female offenders. Correction experts agree that instead of building new prisons, money could be better spent expanding sentencing alternatives for offenders, which help preserve female offenders' families and reduce overcrowding.

The state of Connecticut has made some promising strides in that direction and is now spending $30 million a year on alternative sanctions, including job training, residential programs, drug treatment, and parenting and child care programs. Nearly 20 percent of the five thousand clients of these programs are women. A study released in January 1996 funded by the Justice Education Center, Inc., a nonprofit research group in Hartford, reported that women in alternative incarceration settings, by far, do even better than men. Tracking inmates for two years after their release, the study found that 36 percent of women were arrested after serving an alternative sanction compared with 67 percent of DOC clients. For men it was 51 percent and 52 respectively.

The biggest benefactors, however, may be the children of inmates. Some 75 percent of women in prison are mothers. The National Council on Crime and Delinquency estimated that on any given day in 1991, there were more than 167,000 children in the United States whose mothers were behind bars and that three-fourths of those children were under the age of eighteen. Recent studies have reported that children of inmates are often psychologically traumatized and five to six times more likely than their peers to be incarcerated. I heard more stories than I care to remember about children of inmates in Niantic being tossed from relative to relative, foster home to foster home, or a combination of both. Not all mothers in prison make fit parents, but for those who are or strive to be, more outside drug treatment and parenting skills programs along with steady employment might change such grim dynamics for everyone involved.

William Carbone, who heads the alternative sanctions office under the state's judicial branch, told me that giving women community-based sentences that allowed them daily contact with their children has major repercussions for generations to come. "When women are serving a sentence in the community they learn how to cope with real life, every day situations," he said. "When they're in prison, the children typically develop a lot of hostility because of the instability the separation causes. Then when the mothers are released from prison they too become resentful because they're not used to coping with children."

By the mid-1990s, prison construction nationwide has become a multi-billion dollar industry. Yet by most accounts, it seems reasonable to assume that if confinement and incarceration remain the standard method of punishment, countless families will continue to suffer and the criminal justice system will have made few strides in its efforts to decrease crime. In 1990, David J. Rothman warned as much at the end of his classic treatise on the history of punishment in the United States, *The Discovery of the Asylum*. "We tend to forget that they [penal institutions] were the invention of one generation to serve very special needs," he said, "not the only possible reaction to social problems. . . . We need not remain trapped in inherited answers."

Some final notes: Beatrice Codianni-Robles, who had pleaded guilty to racketeering charges after a sweep of the Latin Kings in the summer of 1994, is now serving a seventeen-year sentence at the federal women's prison in Danbury, Connecticut. At her sentencing hearing in November 1995, Assistant U.S. Attorney Theodore Henrich asked for a ten-year sentence for Codianni-Robles. He explained that she had a unique position in the gang because she did not sell drugs and did not kill anyone. Her attorney, Daniel Schwartz, summoned several witnesses from New Haven's social services community, including the president of the New Haven Board of Aldermen, Tomas Reyes.

But U.S. District Court Judge Alan H. Nevas, a former federal prosecutor, dismissed her community service activities, saying that Codianni-Robles, who was second-in-command of a gang that killed nine people, shot or beat scores of others, and dealt crack and cocaine in New Haven and Bridgeport for most of the 1990s, did not deserve the leniency. "The defendant actively conducted criminal activity behind a veil of social concern," he said. "In doing so, she devastated the community she said she was helping. Families were destroyed and no amount of charitable good work could repair the damage."

In January 1996, Judge Nevas sentenced Nelson Millet, thirty-nine, to life in prison without parole for federal racketeering crimes committed as "the supreme crown president" of the Latin Kings. He became the seventh Latin King sentenced to life. Nevas said he was amazed by Millet's ability to run the gang from a prison three thousand miles away, and pronounced Millet's life "a total waste." Millet at the trial called for the legalization of drugs, to take the profits out of the market so exploited by the Kings and other gangs. Prosecuting attorney Henrich, perplexed by the contradictions in Millet's rhetoric, commented, "The idealism I haven't been able to figure out. It's a mystery to me as to what Mr. Millet's real motives were. . . ."

One recent morning I went to visit Delia Robinson. When I arrived at her house I found her coming off a five-day vodka binge. She looked liked the pernicious character I had heard and written so much about but had never witnessed; it was a sad moment. She looked ashen and swollen. That morning she had been throwing up bile. Gone was the glow of confidence, pumped up by years of prison programs and legions of support. Alone in an apartment most of the time, Delia could no longer muster the strength to keep her monsters at bay and they had returned with a vengeance.

I sat down on a couch across from her as she revealed the obvious. "Andi, I've told you my whole life story and I'm not gonna lie to you. I'm gonna come clean to you now. I've started drinking again." I had known it for some months. The slurred speech over the telephone, the incessant "flus." I had asked her a few times if she'd started drinking and she'd told me she hadn't. She'd renewed a friendship with an old alcoholic friend and they had shared more than a few bouts together. Family members also brought her booze and partied with her.

"I'm in deep trouble, Andi, help me." It was not a role I had anticipated. I called her sponsor from Niantic, Diane Warley, who arrived at Delia's apartment thirty minutes later. Warley had been volunteering at the prison for about twelve years and was now deeply involved in the resettlement program. For the next three hours, Diane prayed with Delia, tried to sober her up and get her thinking straight. Delia cried on and off saying she was having a hard time coping with her son's death. "I could have had lots of grand-babies by now," she said to Warley.

"It's true you've never mourned for Darryl," Warley said. "You carry the guilt and the shame with you all the time. And you've got to start learning to live with the pain. But your problems didn't start with Darryl's death. It goes way back and you need some long-term help."

I made some chamomile tea, about the only thing Delia could get down. Warley started calling around to rehabilitation programs. One program sounded hopeful, but when Warley explained to the coun-selor about Delia's prison record, he put her on hold, then came back on the line and told Warley to call back the next week.

Later in the afternoon, Delia's two nieces from New Haven ar-rived, along with Delia's old friend Libby. The nieces pleaded with Delia to go back with them to New Haven, but Delia resisted. Libby sided with her, saying her friend needed to get well by her own volition. "You just stop being so stupid, girl," she shouted at her. Delia ended up staying at home.

Warley got the runaround from the residential program. She found an AA sponsor for Delia and was trying to get them together, but Delia kept making excuses.

After seeing her that day, I realize how precarious Delia's future on the outside remains. Even the years of rehabilitation in prison could only sustain her temporarily. She had had no professional follow-up, in part because everyone assumed she was unsinkable. In the year and a half Delia had been out of prison, she said her parole officer had visited her once and never phoned her unless she phoned him first.

As I write this, Delia's gone back to work and has regained some of her irrepressible charm. She is back to cooking up a storm for anyone who passes through her doorway and she continues to give tele-phone support to her old friends still at the Farm. Her fall from sobriety may or may not be reparable. I realize the literature on alcoholism says the latter is more likely, but I still try to have hope. Nevertheless, I'm uneasy when I think about her history of alcoholism and how it has gone hand in hand with violence.

This morning on the phone Delia tells me she hasn't gone to any AA meetings and insists she can stay somber on her own. Too many cigarettes have congested her lungs and she wheezes with each breath. She tells me that more than anything she's determined not to fall back "into all the craziness." Seconds pass and I don't say anything. Sensing my concern Delia cuts through the silence by reminding me, "Don't you worry girl, I'm one tough old bird."

In July 1996, Bonnie Foreshaw's petition for Writ of Habeas Corpus was denied by a New London superior court judge. Her lawyer, John Williams, has filed for an appeal.

After working nearly thirty years at the Farm, Elizabeth Gilchrist plans to retire in the spring of 1997.

Acknowledgments

I have many people to thank for contributing to this project, but it was Carol Dunn who made it possible. Convinced that the public might benefit from a book about the realities of incarceration for women, she opened the doors of Niantic to me and allowed me to explore the dimensions of the prison from my own perspective. Even while under tremendous pressure, she met with me regularly and never questioned my motives or tried to sway me to a particular viewpoint. Letting a journalist, with whom she had had little prior contact, inside such a closed society for a prolonged period of time was a courageous act: one that was done with the hope that it might help others.

The staff of Niantic, too numerous to name, provided invaluable guidance. I am especially indebted to Elizabeth Gilchrist, who gave me endless hours of her time, patiently answering my questions, verifying information, and sharing with me her thoughts and insights about working with female inmates. She graciously consented to letting me use photographs of the Farm's early years and allowed me to borrow a number of other items from the archives. Other staff members and volunteers gave generously of their time and were frank and candid with me. They include Diane Sullivan, Mary Benson, Ann Koletsky, Diane Warley, Kathy Mayer, Laura Lago, Beth Racie, Anthony Colonus, Wayne Keck, Doug Vjorn, E. J. Johnson, Liz Martinez, Donna Henry, Ellen Uhlein, and Richard Thomas.

Janet York shared many stories with me about Niantic's history and helped shape my understanding of the various phases in the prison's development. William Wheeler, the assistant director of community relations for the Department of Correction, discussed with me prison policies and the costs of operating the women's prison. The department also allowed me to participate in a week-long workshop for prison staff on the nonviolent approaches used to defuse aggressive behavior.

Then there are the women of Niantic. I spent hundreds of hours with Delia Robinson while she was in prison and after she left. She recapped any number of painful incidents to me, and became a valuable source when it came to explaining inmate behavior. Diane Bartholomew, whose story I could not include in the book, deserves mention. By sharing with me her history as a battered woman and the effects it has had on her daily life, I was able to discard a number of myths I had harbored about the subject. I was deeply moved by the resilience and determination of these two women and by other inmates I met in Niantic. Their stories opened my eyes and enriched my life.

Richard Madden, a veteran reporter and editor at the *New York Times*, supported my articles on the inner city and prisons, which eventually led me to write this book. Sherry Haller of the Justice Education Center, Inc., supplied me with volumes of information on criminal justice issues. Leslie Acoca of the National Council on Crime and Delinquency and Tracy Snell of the Bureau of Justice Statistics gave me useful information concerning the common problems facing women in U.S. prisons.

I was blessed with a fine editor, Clark Dougan. His enthusiasm, patience, and critical eye are the traits every author hopes for. Mickey Rathbun's meticulous and sensitive copyediting made the book a smoother read. My good friend Ted Cheney provided excellent suggestions during the initial drafts of the book. Maureen Kindilien at the Nyselius Library at Fairfield University used her database wizardry to help me narrow down studies on women in prison which suited my theme.

Steven Lewis, a person of strong convictions and generosity, aided me in more ways than he may realize. As my husband, muse, and best friend for nearly twenty years, I am forever grateful for his relentless assurance and comfort. The encouragement of Arthur and Bonnie Lewis and other family members has also meant a great deal to me.

During the course of researching this book, my sister, Kathleen Rierden Nelson, died unexpectedly. As a social worker and family therapist she had worked tirelessly for more than twenty years and in doing so helped to change countless lives for the better. Her compassion and devotion to public service was an inspiration to me. This book is dedicated to her memory.

Selected Bibliography

I collected some of my research from articles dating back thirty years, from the *New York Times*, the *Hartford Courant*, the *Connecticut Post*, the *New Haven Register*, the *New Haven Advocate*, *The Day* of New London, the *Waterbury Republican*, and several local and national magazines including *Atlantic Monthly*, *Harpers*, *Time*, *Newsweek*, and the *New Yorker*. The following is a list of books and reports I found particularly helpful.

Akerstrom, M. "The Social Construction of Snitches." *Deviant Behavior*, 9, 2 (1991): 155–67.

"Alternatives to Incarceration Phase II: Sentencing Evaluation, Year 2." Executive Summary. Prepared by the Justice Education Center, Inc. Hartford, Conn.: Village for Families and Children, January 1996.

American Correctional Association. "The Female Offender: What Does the Future Hold?" American Correctional Association: Laurel, Md., 1990 (booklet).

——. "Female Offenders: Meeting the Needs of a Neglected Population." The American Correctional Association: Laurel, Md., 1993. Contains a range of current studies on issues faced by women inmates.

Biggers, Trisha A. "Death by Murder: A Study of Women Murderers." *Death Education* 3, 1 (Spring 1979): 1–9.

Bloom, Barbara, Russ Immarigeon, and Barbara Owen, eds. "Women in Prisons and Jails." Special issue, *Prison Journal: An International Forum on Incarceration and Alternative Sanctions* 75, 2 (June 1995).

Blount, W. R., and T. A. Danner. "The Influence of Substance Use among Adult Female Inmates." *Journal of Drug Issues* 9, 2 (Spring 1991): 449–67.

Browne, Angela. *When Battered Women Kill*. New York: Free Press, 1987.

Browne, Angela, and K. R. Williams. "Trends in Partner Homicide: A Comparison of Homicides between Marital and Non-Marital Partners for

191

1976–1987." An earlier version of this paper was presented at the American Society of Criminology, Baltimore, Maryland, 1990.

Connecticut Department of Correction. Annual Reports, 1989 through 1994.

Connecticut State Farm for Women. Annual Reports, 1918 through 1940. Housed at the Connecticut State Library in Hartford and at the Niantic Correctional Institution.

Culbert, R. G., and E. P. Fortune. "Incarcerated Women: Self Concept and Argot Roles." *Journal of Offender Counseling, Services and Rehabilitation* 10, 3 (Spring 1986): 25–49.

Fishman, S. "The Impact of Incarceration on the Children of Offenders." *Journal of Children in Contemporary Society* 15, 1 (Fall 1982): 89–99.

Immarigeon, R., and M. Chesney-Lind. "Women's Prisons: Overcrowded and Overused." The National Council on Crime and Delinquency, 1992 (booklet).

Ingram-Fogel, C. "Health Problems and Needs of Incarcerated Women." *Journal of Prison and Jail Health* 10, 1 (Summer 1991): 43–57.

Peace, S. E., C. T. Love, F. B. Hall, and K. L. White. "Evaluation of a Prison-Based Therapeutic Community for Female Substance Abusers." [The Marilyn Baker House]. Central Connecticut State University Department of Sociology/Criminal Justice. February, 1996.

The Permanent Commission on the Status of Women. "Task Force on Women, Children and the Criminal Justice System." Executive Summary. State of Connecticut. January 1989.

Prison and Jail Overcrowding Commission. "Prison and Jail Overcrowding: A Report to the Governor and Legislature." Hartford, Conn.: January 1992.

Rafter, Nicole Hahn. *Partial Justice: Women in State Prisons, 1800–1935*. Boston: Northeastern University Press, 1985.

Rideau, Wilbert, and Ron Wikberg. *Life Sentences: Rage and Survival behind Prison Bars*. New York: Times Books, 1992. An anthology of articles written by inmates at the Louisiana State Prison.

Rogers, Helen W. "The History of the Movement to Establish a State Reformatory for Women in Connecticut." *Journal of Criminal Law and Criminology* 119 (May 1928–February 1929).

Rosen, Ruth. *The Lost Sisterhood: Prostitution in America, 1900–1918*. Baltimore: Johns Hopkins University Press, 1982.

Rothman, David J. *The Discovery of the Asylum: Social Order and Disorder in the New Republic*. Revised Edition. Boston: Little Brown and Co., 1990.

Smith, B., and N. Waring. "The AIDS Epidemic: Impact on Women Prisoners in Massachusetts—An Assessment with Recommendations." *Women and Criminal Justice* 2, 2 (1991): 117–43.

"Street Signs: Gang Culture in the U.S.A." A series of eight articles in part 2 of *Signs of Life in the USA: Readings on Popular Culture for Writers*, edited by Sonia Maasik and Jack Solomon. Boston: St. Martin's Press, 1994.

U.S. Department of Justice. "Special Report: Women in Prison." Washington, D.C.: Bureau of Justice Statistics, March 1991.

U.S. Department of Justice. "Women in Prison: Survey of State Prison In-
    mates, 1991." NCJ-145321. Washington, D.C.: Bureau of Justice Statis-
    tics, 1994.
Viadro, C.I., and J. Earp. "AIDS Education and Incarcerated Women: A
    Neglected Opportunity." *Women and Health* 17 (1991): 105–17.